Fostering Energy

Cherish Your Energy for a Pleasant Spirit

Kyle Pleasant LMT

Copyright © 2021

All Rights Reserved

ISBN: 978-1-7368144-0-6

Table of Contents

Acknowledgments 1

Introduction 3

Section 1: Discover Your Value 6

    Chapter 1: You are Matter Because You Matter 7

    Chapter 2: How It Started 22

    Chapter 3: The Journey to Finding Myself 31

Section 2: Cherishing Your Energy 37

    Chapter 4: How Everything Changed 38

    Chapter 5: Power of Words and Thoughts 49

Section 3: Applying Your Wisdom 60

    Chapter 6: Mental Health 61

    Chapter 7: Physical Health 68

    Chapter 8: Emotional Health 83

    Chapter 9: Spiritual Health 96

    Chapter 10: Being of Service 105

Epilogue: Don't just be inspired; Be inspiring 113

Acknowledgments

I want to thank the late Wayne Dyer and Ernest Holms for giving me the inspiration and the voice to be able to communicate the thoughts and feelings I carried for so many years.

To my best friend Iris, for being the catalyst for change, and for encouraging me to follow my passion and not be tied to conventional wisdom. For challenging me to follow my dreams no matter what others think.

To my mother Gayle, for raising me with the values and beliefs that have carried me to be the best of myself. For my objectivity and intuition as well as independence to not just be someone that was held back because I couldn't see so well, but to overcome obstacles and be my own person.

For my father Frank, even though we didn't quite see eye to eye during my adolescent years, we finally found our way when we have become older and wiser. I take comfort in knowing there is mutual respect and admiration for each other's journey in life.

To my wife and partner of 13 years for standing by me, with words of encouragement and the confidence that I could carry us through new adventures.

To my daughter Khloe, the apple of my eye. Always there with joy in her heart and a smile on her face. With the wisdom well beyond her years.

Introduction

A passage that hangs on my front door reads, "Please be responsible for the energy you bring into this home." Along with others on my walls, this quote serves as a reminder not only to guests but to me. We are all energy, and should all be held responsible for what we drag along with us. Our energy has an immense impact on our surroundings, and the sooner we can understand this, the sooner we can use it positively.

Fostering Energy introduces the idea that everything we do impacts those around us, both people and objects alike. In this book, I share how energy surrounds everyone, so it must be taken care of. We are all responsible for our energies. I am energy, and so are you!

Energy is so much more than what powers our homes. Everyone and everything has energy, both positive and negative. These words are energy vibrations themselves! When we interact with the world and socialize with people, a transaction of energy waves occurs. Every single interaction we make, no matter how small, has an impact on our personal energy, and our energy has an impact on everything around us. It's a never-ending cycle, yet the importance of fostering energy goes vastly understated.

Fostering often brings forth an image of raising a child. To foster a child means to promote their personal growth and development and to cherish them as an individual. Our energy requires the same nurture and care as a child does. When we come into our human forms, we are given a charge of energy. This is a great responsibility and one that is taken far too lightly by most people. By fostering our energy, we can promote personal growth and development and shield ourselves from negative influence.

If this is your first time hearing about personal energy, don't be overwhelmed! I've structured this book in a way that encourages newcomers to the topic but still provides deep insight into truly fostering your energy. The first step of the book is a reflection exercise on self-worth. To get the most out of fostering our energy, it is crucial to understand that we all have value. You have value.

Once we've all agreed that every single one of us has worth, we can transition into the next step of the process. Recognizing that you not only have value but so does the energy you carry can take some time to wrap your head around. Energy is special, and if it is nurtured and fostered healthily, it can do incredible things.

The third and final step in my book is the application of this knowledge. Just like in school, understanding the theories and facts is fine and dandy, but it's not until the information is put into action that it all comes together. Drawing inspiration from I *Dare You* by William Danforth, this final section walks through methods to improve mental, physical, spiritual, and emotional health all while being of service to those around you.

I invite you to join me on a journey you won't soon forget. *Fostering Energy* teaches a crucial skill, not just for your health and self-worth but for those around you. By taking control of the energy you bring with you and wherever you go, every interaction made, whether at the grocery store, coffee shop, or even at home, will be much more enjoyable for everyone involved.

Learning to foster my energy has changed my life, and I know yours will change too.

Section 1
Discover Your Value

Chapter 1
You are Matter Because You Matter

"If you're struggling today, remember that life is worth living and believe that the best is yet to come. Remember that you are loved, you matter, and never forget that there is always hope."

- Germany Kent

Have you ever been so distressed and exhausted that you just wanted to give up on everything? If you have, you are not alone in this experience. We all have been through similar experiences and feelings at some point in our lives. It is normal to feel anxious and stressed at times. However, something is wrong when it takes over everything you need to do or everything that you are.

When this happens, these negative feelings will eat away at you and rob you of your peace of mind. Before I go into further details about this chapter and book, I need to tell you one thing: You are special, and you matter.

Yes, you read that correctly. You are special, and the very fact that you were sent into this world is proof enough that you matter. So if you ever feel useless, just know that this feeling is temporary, and remind yourself that God must have sent you down here for a reason. He does not do things without reason.

We, as humans, are here in this world because we have a particular purpose to serve. Whenever I voice this to people around me, they always ask me how they can know what their life purpose is. I always answer their question by telling them, "You know it very well."

And yes, we do. We all know what the purpose of our lives is; we are just not aware of it. Thus, we feel as though we don't know it. Individual peoples' purposes will always be different.

You have to make the best out of this chance of existence that you've been given and fulfill your purpose. It's true; we all have a purpose but all of us will fulfill it, simply because some individuals refuse to discover themselves and their values. Does that sound perplexing? Here's another way I'll help you understand.

Close your eyes, and ask yourself, "What is the one thing that I want most, in life?"

Your answers may be;
I want a big house;
I want a good job;
I want a loving life partner;
I want a luxurious car;
I want peace;

I want a caring family;

And so on. Now, when you express that you want a big house, a good job, or a loving spouse, your primary purpose is not getting a house, job, or spouse. These are just sources that will serve your primary purpose. What will you achieve when you attain a big house, a good job, or a loving partner? You will experience happiness; contentment; satisfaction.

So, the ultimate reasoning behind every desire of ours is to feel happy and content, which is a natural state. This is what our life's purpose is – to be happy and to be able to spread that happiness and peace. We don't realize it because every day, we are excessively consumed by our worrying thoughts. Why do the hardships and tribulations that occur during life bother you? They disturb your peace and happiness. The only thing we all live for in this world is happiness and peace.

Even though that is what we all live for, we don't know how to achieve it. And this is the reason we become troubled and remain that way. When we are distressed, we begin to emit negative energy into our surroundings, and chaos ensues. In the upcoming chapters, I will mention a lot about energy and its role in our life. However, as of now, let's continue to simply stay focused on life's purpose.

In my life, I have come across many people that have told me that they know their ultimate purpose in life is to be happy and to spread happiness, but that they can't find true, real happiness.

I know of many people who have everything they want in their lives, yet are still not happy. Why? Because they perceive their entire worth and value based on other people's opinions about them. They are so busy trying to please people around them in an effort to get their approval, that they don't remember or have time to love themselves.

When we constantly live our lives to meet other individuals' expectations of us, we will always, *always* end up feeling disappointed and neglected. We are placing our value and worth into the hands of someone who doesn't have the time or energy to satisfy your need for approval.

This is the reason why so many people go blank when they talk about the purpose in their lives. They know that they want to be happy, but they can't be even after achieving what they want because they try to find their happiness in others. An example of this would be;

Let's suppose your favorite color is yellow. You bought a new yellow shirt that you liked, in an online store. You plan to wear it on your birthday that is just around the corner. You're excited along with your birthday. On the day, you wear that shirt, take a picture, and post it on your social media. You are waiting for your friends to compliment your picture. Just then, a notification pops up and you open it.

"I think this color doesn't go with your complexion," a friend had commented. Within a fraction of a second, all your excitement fades. Suddenly, you start hating yourself. You remove the picture and decide to never wear the shirt again. Just a comment like that has damaged your self-esteem. You feel hurt and upset and think your friend shouldn't have said that. But is the person to blame your friend? If you think like this, you need to make some changes to your thought process. Yes, no one should say anything, especially not about ones' looks, unless it is helpful or nice. But in this situation, it is you that is letting this happen. If you believe you like something, then like it fully. Why do you need others' validation about your choice in the first place? Why do you let your life be defined by other peoples' opinions? Opinions are meant to be different and that is why they are known as opinions. You can't expect someone's opinion to be the same as yours all the time.

To some people, playing video games is a good way to pass time and have fun, whereas some other people think playing video games is a waste of time. If you like playing them and you find yourself amidst video game haters, valuing yourself based on their opinions would be a senseless decision to make.

Depression, anxiety, and other mental illnesses are much more prevalent now than they were decades ago. This is partly because there is more awareness around the topic; meaning more people suffering from such illnesses can get diagnoses and get the help that they need without as much stigma. But, the emergence of more anxiety and stress-related illnesses can also because we, as humans and individuals have become so much more public, adding to our stresses. Our lives have become public due to the emergence of social media.

We are so vulnerable that we get affected by everyone's opinion of us. I know of many people who are gifted with remarkable talents yet they are still not successful in their lives because they live their lives based on society's approval.

Take this as a reminder to remember that you *cannot* please everyone, nor is it your responsibility to. There will always be some people who will never like you, no matter what you do. It should be something that you do not even bother concerning yourself with.

Your primary responsibility is to determine your real worth and value and to keep yourself happy and at peace. As I mentioned earlier, the true purpose of our lives is to be happy and to spread happiness in this world. To get to that final step, we need to be happy ourselves. We need to have had achieved absolute inner peace.

I know your life may not be easy, but maybe full of trials, misfortunes, and troubling experiences. I understand it very much so. I know that sometimes, you may feel like giving up and never getting back up again, but the truth is, hardships and the misfortunes present in our lives can sometimes shape us for the better, or teach us to be stronger. They can teach us to deal with challenges and teaches us emotional as well as physical growth. I know that this belief system cannot be applied to every terrible experience, but to even have this outlook while approaching trouble or while working through past experiences, can be very helpful and calming for your mind and peaceful. In a way, you may be a piece of coal currently under a lot of pressure. In a while, the pressure will lift, and you will no longer be just a piece of coal. You will be a hard-earned diamond.

So the purpose of trials and tribulations can sometimes be to make you strong or resilient. Just like you, my life was, and it still is, full of adversities. And I am content. Not because I am different from you, or special, but because I learned how to accept my challenges. When I embraced my problems, I realized that they were not as tormenting as they initially seemed to be. And this is the message that I want to spread throughout this book. I want you to know, that whatever it is you're running away from, you should stop and face it. I want individuals like yourself to read this book and feel like you can face your problems, and deal with them with emotional maturity and growth.

I want to spread peace and happiness in this world. And I want you to know that you are essential and always will be.

There is no one out there that is like you. You are the only one.

No one can even come close to being like you. You possess some fantastic strengths and talents that no one else does. What you do, can never be copied or done in the same way as you. That is what makes you unique.

What you've gone through and survived, are also unique to you. Only you will ever know what going through and surviving them means and feels like. Some of these unique experiences have taught you and are also unique to yourself. You have turned into someone that needs to be heard; as you should. Every single person out there has a voice that they just need to look for.

Become a storyteller. Take the lessons you've worked through and share them with people around you. You're the only one that has been through them, and the world needs your contribution. Help them learn from those experiences, and find strength in being with people that are also constantly looking to better themselves and find themselves.

You have a destiny and purpose that only you can fulfill.

Deep down, you are aware of this. You are just fearful of failure. So remember that failure is a blessing in disguise; it allows you to learn. Therefore, never let your fear hold you back. You have so much ahead of you, you may have a unique career, a unique family life, unique passions, unique goals, an exceptional personality, which means that *no one* will ever experience even a day of your life in your shoes.

Your dreams and goals are your destiny and can only be accomplished by you. When you work towards pursuing these dreams, you create an impact on many lives. Your dreams are guided and supported by your passion. There is one thing you are passionate about. You must find it and be determined in your passion to achieve your dreams. It is inside of you, just waiting to be found.

Don't compare your failures, your struggles, or even your accomplishments to those of others. We each have our journeys and struggles in life. So, focus on your life and strive to make it better.

Your Love Matters For Your Loved Ones

There are a bunch of people in your life that you genuinely care about and love. They might be your parents, siblings, spouse, kids, and friends. The rest of the world doesn't feel the way that you do, about them. You are important because only you have the potential to love them unconditionally, the way that you do. Love is the best gift, and it is one of the biggest reasons for happiness. Nothing is comparable to it. Giving that love for others is what makes life most meaningful.

The purest achievements in life don't come from helping the masses but from helping the people around you. The most affectionate people are the ones who make their friends and family feel important and happy. You are that person for them! You can influence your loved ones' lives more than anyone else can in the world.

You Are Meant to Improve

Throughout the journey of life, we are supposed to continuously learn and grow. Unfortunately, some people never realize this fact and stop pushing themselves forward. The good news is, you are not one of those people, because if you were, you wouldn't be reading this book; the fact that you picked this book up shows that you have an urge to improve yourself. And this urge will help you move forward. Those who try, certainly succeed one day. You are a person who wants to find ways to turn yourself into your most brilliant version possible. Through the quest of self-mastery, you will reach your highest potential, which will be of even more significance than you are today.

You Are Special for Someone

There is at least one person in this world that truly adores you. Yes, you read it correctly. They may be a parent, child, sibling, spouse, friend, or co-worker. You are truly important in their eyes, and they can't imagine their lives without you, and they never want to, either. They care for you and your wellbeing.

Some things, like being loved by another, should never be underestimated because even though it may seem insignificant at times, it can be the biggest difference there can be, between giving up and continuing to persevere. You have every right to feel proud. The fact that you mean so much to someone else is a big honor and responsibility.

Instead of caring about people who are least bothered about your existence, start living your life for those who adore you. Unfortunately, in this virtual age, people tend to neglect their families and loved ones for online friendships. But you are not one of them. You care for your loved ones; therefore, you are reading this book so that you can bring a positive change in your life. Only you have the power to give that same love back to them. Your love will be the most treasured. It will mean the most to this person if it comes from you than from anyone else.

Discovering your value is all about knowing your worth, believing in yourself, and working towards high self-esteem, rather than wallowing in low self-worth.

Self-esteem and self-respect do go together. It has to do with how you value yourself, as I've said. Please take note of the fact that it is a feeling. Self-esteem is not an intellectual equation that can be solved. You must be emotionally mature, or working to be, to get to where you need to be. That is why people also talk about how you view yourself emotionally.

In short: it is a sense of what you are worth. Self-esteem has to do with self-awareness as well. It is, therefore, also the degree to which you have respect for yourself. The feelings we have towards ourselves influence how we live our lives and how we see ourselves in our minds; how we may judge ourselves for our actions.

People who feel loved and appreciated (in other words, people with high self-esteem) have better social relationships. They are more likely to ask friends and family for help and support when they need it. Everything is connected when it comes to how you perceive yourself and how you value yourself.

People who believe they can achieve their goals and solve problems tend to do better in school. Achieving higher self-esteem allows you to accept yourself and live life to the full extent, without berating yourself over every single thing.

Steps to Discover Your Value

If you want to discover your value, improve your self-esteem. Here are some tips to get started:

Stop having negative thoughts about yourself. If you are used to focusing on your flaws, start thinking about positive aspects that offset them. When you find yourself being overly critical of yourself, counter it by saying something positive about yourself. Each day writes down three things about yourself that make you happy.

Aim for achievement rather than perfection. Some people end up paralyzed due to their desire for perfection. Instead of holding yourself back with thoughts like, "I'm not going to try and start my own business until I have enough money," think about what you're good at and what you enjoy and go for it.

See mistakes and failures as learning opportunities. Accept that you *will* make mistakes because everyone makes them, one way or another. Mistakes are a part of the experience; they are a part of the learning process. Remember that a person's skills are continually developing and that everyone excels at different things and different paces — it's what makes people interesting.

When my wife and I got our first house a few years ago, we wanted to fix it up. I didn't know anything about home repair. I watched a few YouTube videos, hung out at the Home Depot asked a lot of questions and before long I was painting rooms, changed out wall outlets and the landscape of my whole yard.

Always try new things. Experiment with different activities that put you in touch with your skills. Then be proud of the new skills you have acquired, and work on those skills more.

Identify what you can change and what you cannot. If you realize that something about you does not make you happy and you can change it, start now. If it's something that you cannot change (like your height), start working on loving yourself just the way you are. Look at what continues to show up in your life. Perhaps what is being shown to you is where you are out of alignment with your peace.

Set goals. Think about what you would like to achieve and then come up with a plan to do it. Stick to the plan and see your recorded progress. Be proud of your opinions and ideas. Don't be afraid to express them. Collaborate in social work. Help clean up your neighborhood, participate in a charity marathon for a good cause, or volunteer for a homeless shelter. You will feel differently; better about yourself, when you're contributing to something in society, and that your help is recognized; it works wonders to increase self-esteem.

Have fun, and don't take everything so seriously. Have you ever found yourself thinking things like: "I would have more friends if I were able to let go once in a while?"

Enjoy spending your time with people you care about and doing something that you love. Relax and have a good time — and don't put your life on hold.

The thousands of impressions, evaluations, and experiences, thus gathered come together in a positive feeling towards ourselves or, on the contrary, in an uncomfortable feeling of not being what we expected. The concept that we have of ourselves is not something inherited, but learned from around us, through the assessment we make of our behavior and the assimilation and internalization of others' opinions about us. If you continue to internalize the opinions of others then you must ask yourself - where do they end and where do you begin? We must come to a place where those internalized thoughts start to reflect what the higher self sees for yourself.

If you are using others to measure your value, consider where that option is coming from in the first place. There are people out there struggling to find their peace and are just as lost. Why would you want to ask them for directions?

The importance of self-esteem lies in the fact that it drives us to act, to move forward, and motivate us to pursue and achieve our goals. It is never too late to build positive and healthy self-esteem to discover your real value.

Self-esteem plays a role in almost everything you do. People with high self-esteem do better in school and find it easier to make friends. They tend to have better relationships with people their age and with adults, are happier and have less trouble dealing with mistakes, disappointments, and failures, and are more likely to stick with something until they do it. It takes some work, but it's a skill you'll have for life; you'll eventually know your worth and discover your value.

I have a saying on my front door that says "Please be responsible for the energy you bring into this home."

This quote along with others I have on the inside walls of my house serve as reminders that I am energy and I am responsible for how I show up when I come into my home each day and how to show up when I go out into the world as well as reminders for others entering my house. These words are energy vibrations themselves. Pictures, television, books, the people we socialize with, all have energy and operate on a specific vibration.

Chapter 2
How It Started

There are many people that want to achieve different goals in their lives. We all face all sorts of obstacles which some may think of as the universe being out to get them, and others may think of as tests to help them become the best versions of themselves.

Much like everyone else, I had my own goal of becoming someone. I wanted to become happy. Happiness is something that many people lack when they claim to do something they love. Those around us always talk about what they want to do and where they want to be and despite struggling for most of their lives, they still don't manage to attain happiness. Sure, we all have those surges of happiness, like when we first buy something off of our own money or when we hear our favorite songs. Or even if we find forgotten change in the pockets of our old jeans.

There's happiness in every speck of our being, yet we are rarely ever able to see a happy big picture.

Much like all these people, I, too, once felt the same. Not realizing where like would take me was one of the most daunting tests that life put me through. Yes, I am not a billionaire, but I can assure you that at this moment, as I'm writing this, I am much happier than those billionaires combined.

Today, I am a massage therapist. I celebrated my 8th year as one and it brings me immense joy to be where I am today.

For any person to achieve anything in their lives, however small or big it may be, takes a lot of courage. I am here today to not only acknowledge the courage of every person in this world but also to applaud it.

Looking back and how far I've come, makes me realize just how long and meaningful my journey has been. While this book is more focused on my journey and my story, I hope everyone reading this can take a walk down this road with me.

As some may or may not know, I am legally blind. I was born with cataracts in both eyes and while in this day and age, surgery for cataracts is widespread, in 1974, it wasn't. The best that they can do back then was to surgically remove the clouded lenses from the eyes, which, in my experience, renders one blind. So when I was born, I had two options, either A) be blind or B) be blind. And you won't even believe the option I chose. A cataract, by definition, is a medical condition where the lens of one's eye progressively gets opaque which results in blurred vision.

You must be wondering how I manage to see well enough to be able to choose a profession of a massage therapist. Well, the answer is, I don't.

I do have some vision left which was the result of removing clouded lenses from my eyes, but it doesn't enable me to see as much. Most of what I can see are fuzzy figures and my mind is left with the mystery of figuring out just what these fuzzy figures can be. It could be a table, a car, or even a person, and it's not until I feel the thing or the person speaks up, am I able to conclude what it is.

If you think that's unfortunate, let me tell you a bit more. In 1993, when I was around the age of 19, I underwent retinal detachment surgery in my right eye. A retinal detachment surgery is a condition in which a thin layer of tissue, which is the retina, at the back of the eye pulls away from its normal position. In this condition, what happens is that the retinal cells are separated from the layer of blood vessels which inhibits the oxygen from reaching the eye.

This particular surgery left me with a loss of vision in my right eye and an extremely fuzzy left one.

However, I still managed to go to regular school albeit with great difficulties, but I managed to adapt to my surroundings.

Let rewind a bit. Going to school and making new friends had always been a challenge. It had been a challenge not for me, rather for other people. I was always labeled as "that blind kid" in school, and it felt as though there was not a single way I could make it past that label. My disability became a defining factor for who I was as a person.

Most of the kids my age didn't look at me as a funny kid or witty kid. They looked at me as the one with a disability. In hushed whispers, I always found the mention of my name when I walked by a group of friends. It came to the point where everyone automatically assumed that due to my disability, I would also have anti-social tendencies.

Well, I didn't. People just didn't approach me enough. It became a chore being treated as though I'm a ceramic doll, and with one wrong touch, I would break into a million pieces. I wasn't one. I longed to be treated the same as others and I would've given anything to not be defined by my disability.

Among the sea of people for whom I was just that blind kid, I had the support of my mother. Despite having a son with such a grave disability, my mother never failed to treat me normally. From a young age, she had taught me to be independent. She reminded me that I am so much more than my disability.

My mother was the one person who believed in my abilities. She enabled me to be able to see a sight that many people with eyes fail to see. The sight of true happiness and content.

Much like other young kids, studies were a different obstacle for me. With the help of my teachers, I was able to not lack in my class. I still remember that unlike in today's world, audiobooks were not commonly used. I remember having to ask someone else to help me read things if there wasn't a large-print version of my textbooks. That is when I even decided to use them.

Unlike other kids, I couldn't do most of the things. Like I couldn't participate in any sort of sports or even ground play with other kids. It was hard for me to be able to play with kids my age sometimes, they didn't understand the concept of someone having a disability. And for those that did get past my disability, their curious little minds had many questions, ready to be asked.

Even in this day and age, many people wonder how I manage my daily life routine. Truth is, when you're this old and had been living with a disability ever since you're born, it grows on you. Besides, it's not like I had any other option. I mean life isn't an interactive book where God gives you options such as 'if you choose to be legally blind, turn to page number 64. If not, continue reading'. As much as we wish we had control over situations like these, we don't.

I never let my disability define me. To others, I may have been labeled as the blind kid but to myself, I knew I was much more than that. And at the end of the day, what I thought about myself mattered far more than what other people think.

There is a saying that I am reminded of, as I write this and it goes something like this

"Happiness grows at our fireside, and is not to be picked from strangers gardens" - Douglas Jerrold

The message that I take away from this quote is that every individual is capable of finding happiness in themselves, in their surroundings. Although we may not be able to control certain things in our lives, we do have control over how we perceive our situations. For example, growing up, I stopped counting my scars and focused more on my stars.

I knew very well that I may never be able to drive a car or fly a plane of even so much as observing a peaceful night of staring at the stars, but this doesn't mean that I would dismiss the things that I can do.

Contrary to popular belief, I was quite an introvert. This gave me the ability to be able to connect with people who didn't deduce me down to my disability. Learning from my disability, I also managed to develop an extra sense of empathy that I have seen many abled people lack. Using my traits such as these, I tried to focus more on what I can do with this and how can I utilize these traits in a positive, more helpful, manner.

Since the profession of blind motivational speakers wasn't at its peak back then, I had to choose a much different career path.

I landed my first "real job" at a non-profit paper manufacturing company. This was right after I graduated college. The paper manufacturing company had a percentage of vacancies specifically for blind people, so I, fortunately enough, had the perfect disability for that.

Despite lacking a sense of sight, I believe that I was particularly smart. I saw opportunities in places other people saw distress. For an average person, working at a paper manufacturing company isn't the dream job, which leads them to be as demotivated as possible. But not me. No, I never looked at it that way. Well, at least not during the start of it.

Working in this company, I saw the opportunity of learning how to use the computer, and I jumped at the chance and availed it.

In those times, learning how to use the computer was a skill that gave me more of an edge. It was right around the time when things were slowly, but surely, changing towards a more technical world. People were easing into the idea of digitizing their work and learning how to do just that, making things easier for me. So, for the next eight years, I worked as the company's IT person. I had the job of helping people fix their printers, scanners or even helping people change their emails.

The job, at that time, seemed sufficient enough in terms of finances. It paid pretty well and money wasn't an active concern for me. All my bills were able to smoothly go by and I was able to have 3 sufficient meals on my table each day. I had a great rapport built with my colleagues and I managed to fit right in with everyone else.

Despite all this, a part of me felt incomplete. I felt as though I was meant to do something else, something different. And even though it looked like I was fitting right in with the rest of the puzzle pieces, I couldn't help but shake the feeling that maybe I wasn't the right fit. Almost like I belong somewhere else, but I have been shaped to fit among the people with whom I did not belong.

For a while, I tried to fight the feeling. For a person living with a major limitation, a stable job, appropriate workplace, and food on the table should be what matters the most, but somehow, it didn't. I felt like I was lacking something. As if I was somewhere where I no longer belonged to.

Don't get me wrong, I cherish the time I spent there and the people I met. More importantly, I cherish the things I learned there but deep down I knew I was meant to do something different. Something that made me feel as though my purpose in life was being fulfilled.

My days at the paper manufacturing company started feeling monotonous, almost as if I was on auto-pilot. Each day seemed to be the same with minor differences of its own. With each passing day, my hunger for learning more and doing more grew. And every day, I felt a little less like myself and a little more like someone was forcing me to be.

Like I was a puzzle piece of who was shaving its edges just so it could fit with the other pieces. It was then when I realize that I didn't need to shave my edges. I was different. I was unique, and

I was eager to discover myself more and more. I didn't need to fit in because I knew that I couldn't. I was, at the end of the day, living with a disability and although it never became a defining label for myself in my eyes, it did set me aside from everyone else. Not in an "I'm disabled" way, but more in an "I'm differently-abled" way.

Chapter 3
The Journey to Finding Myself

"Have the courage to follow your heart and intuition. They somehow already know what you truly want to become."

-Steve Jobs

After spending eight significant years at "The Lighthouse," I decided that it was time to part my ways. Those eight years gave me a lot to learn along with friendships I never thought I would have. But it was time for me to move forward with my life; with my goals.

I know my disability may seem like a limitation to most people, but to me, it wasn't. I left my previous job because I didn't feel like I was making a real difference in the world. Well, aside from fixing people's printers or changing their emails. I wanted to do more for the world, and not get caught up in office politics or get lost in the daily grind.

For a moment though, I felt lost. There was also a part of me who was second-guessing the decision I just made. I mean, having a stable paycheck was something that anybody would second guess before leaving, but I had to remind myself of the bigger picture.

I didn't know what to do or where to go at first, so I decided to take a break from everything and make a journey towards finding myself. When a person is in that stage of life nothing seems to make sense, it's always better to detach yourself from it. This happens because oftentimes when we think and over-think about something too much, our brain starts to treat it as something 'boring'. Have you ever spent so much time studying for a test and when it's time for that test, and you're skimming through your notes, your brain tends to overlook things because "I already know this"? This is precisely why taking a break is important. More often than not, our brains tend to overlook things and it isn't after we take a small break, are we able to see things from a different perspective. Einstein said, "You can't solve a problem with the same mind that created it."

For this exact reason, I took a year off to go backpacking across Europe and hiking the Appalachian Trail. You know, the usual stuff you do when you are trying to "find yourself". I don't know if it was due to spending so much time in nature, or because it was such a vastly different environment for me, but I learned a lot about myself on those trails. I developed an even deeper connection with the world, and that helped me become who I am today.

I've always had somewhat of a nurturing aspect to my personality and getting out seeing the world allowed me to develop it from a different perspective. There was something about spending time in nature with such closed proximity, which gave me an even deeper insight in regards to the world around me. It was during this time in my life that I chose to begin massage school. The school that I went to was very hands-on and got me excited about my new profession. Fortunately, they were able to work with me one on one where I was having trouble because of my limited eyesight. It took only a very short time for my new skills to seem completely natural to me, and by the time I graduated, it was like I had been doing massage for my whole life.

After I got my license in Texas, I worked in the student clinic for about 7 months. Each state in our great Union has a different feel to it, and I found it more challenging to be accepted as a massage therapist in Texas because I was male. I chose to temporarily return to the computer industry and moved to Arkansas to get my networking degree. Some of you might think this was a step backward. Instead, it turned out to be the best decision I ever made, because it was during this time that I met my wife Kelsey.

After I graduated, we decided to move to Oregon because Intel was up there and we also had great transportation since neither of us drive. This was in 2008 when the recession was in full swing, and good openings in IT were scarce. Since we were in a new community with more open-minded people, I decided to give massage therapy another try. So, in 2013 I went back to massage school for another year, at East West College. I was again blessed with instructors that were able to work with my visual impairment so that I could graduate with all the skills I needed.

I have been working as a massage therapist for several years now, and just last year, I started my practice out of my house which I named Pleasant Touch Massage. I have had the joy to meet and work with some wonderful people over these years that have helped make this business a success. My wife Kelsey and I, as well as our 3-year-old daughter Khloe at that time, moved to a new home this past summer, and I am now working on putting my practice in the extra workspace we have.

As far as my blindness is concerned, I don't feel that has hindered me. Sure, I have a little more of a challenge than most people in using a computer, so it takes me a little longer to make notes or appointments for my clients. I've always been adaptable, and technology is making it even easier for me to interact with the tools we use on a daily basis.

I believe that my blindness gives me unique skills that allow me to excel as a massage therapist. I believe that because of the vision loss, my sense of touch, as well as my intuition is heightened. I've often been told by clients that I end up finding trigger points, painful knots, and areas of tension on them that they didn't even know about. I pretty much let my hands do the communicating during every session.

But it wasn't always like that. In my adolescent years and early 20's, I was distracted by the idea of finding someone; a girlfriend. For some reason, I thought that if I have a relationship, I was going to feel more complete. Back then, I was young and naïve. The concept of not needing "a better half" because I was already whole was something that I was not familiar with. This feeling was so intense that when I went to college, I attached myself to the first woman who I got close to, and ended up marrying her. This could have been because somewhere deep down, I was also labeling myself as my disability, and thought that the first opportunity I get of finding love, I should take it. During that time, it didn't occur to me that I am just as much worthy of love as anyone else and that if I were to find love, I would find it regardless of anything. The marriage didn't last more than a year because my wife of that time wasn't able to fully devote her attention towards us. Once that marriage had failed, I started feeling the lack of intimate relationships even more. So much so that I continued to seek out a relationship that was far from being healthy for me, to the point where I contemplated committing suicide whenever any one of those ended.

I desperately sought out a relationship without even thinking that having them would not complete me simply because I was never half to begin with. I just need to make myself realize that I am just as whole as anyone else and that not having intimate relationships does not define my worth. It was not after a few years went by, after traveling and soul searching that I had gotten to a place where the relationship with myself was the most important one for me and I found value in myself. It was then that I realized that having a relationship wasn't as important as people made it out to be.

When I finally did find love, it was when I was ready for it, not when I was desperate for it. Love showed up when I least expected it to, and finally, I realized that I didn't have to compromise on who I was or what I was doing. I was able to have a healthy and happy relationship with my wife, where both of us knew that neither of us completed each other; we were two complete individuals who decided to spend the rest of their lives together.

Many people are labeled as having a disability, and that label can be more disabling than the disability itself. If I had just one piece of advice to give to anyone who has a disability or doubts their abilities, it is this: Trust your gut and your instincts. If there is something you want to do, don't let those voices in your head (or the well-meaning voices of friends and family) distract you. Just go for it! You can find a way, or you can make a way. You never know what you can do unless you try. You'll be surprised at what happens next.

Section 2
Cherishing Your Energy

Chapter 4
How Everything Changed

"Emotions are what make us human. Make us real. The word 'emotion' stands for energy in motion. Be truthful about your emotions, and use your mind and emotions in your favor, not against yourself"

-Robert T. Kiyosaki.

We all have been through thick and thin in our lives. And during those times, our bodies have a certain mechanism in which they react to our emotions. For instance, you are in the examination hall with all your friends and the exam is about to begin in a few minutes. All of your friends will go to their given seats and so will you. How do you feel at that moment when you are just parting with your friends, not to mention the anxiety about the exam? Several questions pop up in your mind. Will the exam be easy? Will I be able to do well? What if I don't pass the exam? How will my parents react? Will my friends do better than me? You have this adrenaline rushing through your body, you are sweating, your heart is racing, your legs trembling. That's precisely the energy you are resonating at that moment.

Our emotions are energy. Now, what do we know about energy? Probably the first thing that comes to mind is that energy is never destroyed, it transforms from one form to another. The light energy enables the plant to convert the light energy into chemical energy and synthesize food. The apple you eat in the morning before going to work has the chemical energy that is converted into mechanical energy in your body. And so on, the mechanical energy then enables you to do physical tasks and mental work.

Emotions are just the same as energy. They move, they keep changing, they have a frequency, they take forms and they are temporary. Emotions are what we experience throughout the day. Emotions are temporary states that influence our bodies and our behavior. Love is what you experience when someone shows you kindness. Anger is what you experience when you are stuck in a traffic jam while you are late for work. Anxiety is what you experience when you have to present in front of the whole class. Love, anger, and anxiety; all these are emotions. Emotions that influence our lives.

Emotions are transient in their very nature. Any emotion cannot last for very long. This moment you may be ecstatic, and then the next moment you may be upset. This moment you may be empathetic, then a while later, you might be rude. In another moment you may be optimistic and still another moment you may be worried. This pendulum of emotions keeps moving from one feeling to another.

Many people tell me that they don't feel anything, that they are just numb, that they have ceased to have an emotional response to anything. You might see this as a contradiction to what I said above about emotions being a regular part of our lives. But one thing to be pointed out here is that going numb is also an emotion. It's a traumatic response to an adverse situation.

Emotions are never the same. You have never experienced an emotion that has lasted long. You have never had an emotion that stayed its course and never faded. You have never felt a permanent emotion.

"Everything in life is vibration."

—**Albert Einstein**

Emotions are vibrations. A vibration is a state of being, the atmosphere, or the energetic quality of a person, place, thought, or thing. Emotions are also like a compass, they help you navigate to whether you are in alignment, in harmony with your source. Just like physical pain in the body, emotions are a warning system that helps bring you back to peace.

You must be perplexed to read emotions are vibrations. However, let's back-track it a little so that we can come back to this conclusion.

We all have had the chance to attend a chemistry class at some point in our lives. You must remember learning something about atoms, that everything is made up of atoms and that atoms are the basic and the smallest unit that any matter can be divided into. Atoms together make molecules and therefore, we may say that everything around us is a combination of atoms.

As you experience it yourself, you realize that the entire material world is nothing but vibration. When we witness the ocean of infinite waves surging within. When we listen to the river of inner sensations flowing within, the eternal dance of the countless vibrations within every atom of the body. That's when we realize the constantly changing nature in front of us. All of this is happening at an extremely subtle level. As you begin to understand the reality of matter to be vibration, you also start experiencing the reality of the mind: consciousness, perception, sensation, and certainly, emotions.

Everything, without a doubt, in the universe is vibrating at its frequency. The chair or the couch you are sitting on may not seem to be vibrating to you right now, but think of it this way. The atoms and collectively, the molecules in your chair are in a constant state of motion, continuously oscillating in the given area. And because the vibration of those molecules is so condensed due to the compactness of the chair, you are sitting calmly on it without having to worry about its vibration.

Emotions, work in the same way to a large extent. Emotions resonate with the vibrational frequency that they bring about.

The higher the vibrational frequency, the higher the expansion, and the greater the energy in your body cells. The lower the vibrational frequency, the greater the contraction, and the lesser of the vital energy in your cells.

For instance, when you are vibrating at a higher level, you feel and more at ease, in rhythm with your consciousness. Even the problems seem easy to deal with, as you feel lighter as if a burden has been taken off your shoulders. However, lower vibrations feel heavy and full of turmoil. Almost all spiritual practices point the way toward higher realms of consciousness, and recent researches have even quantified the vibrations of different states of being to create a scale of consciousness.

To quote a few, enlightenment has the highest frequency of 700+ and the greatest expansion of energy. The vibrational frequency of joy is 540 and is expansive. However, when we experience something undesirable, the vibrational frequency falls below 200 and results in contraction.

After decades of research and extensive historical studies, Quantum Physics also proves that physical matter doesn't exist, that everything is just energy-carrying different frequencies of vibration. Because of the varying frequencies of energy, we see all the different creations in the world around us. For instance, the grass and the flowers, the trees, and the clouds, all have different frequencies of energy and so we these things as different and not one.

Once we get accustomed to the idea of everything being a form of energy and possessing vibrational frequencies, it becomes easier to understand that life is more of an energy system that's a collection of materialistic things. That means that if we are conscious of our actions, the emotions we experience are the energy they contain, we can make conscious decisions about how to control and improvise that energy.

If you are feeling frustrated and are also aware of what that negative energy is doing to your well-being and your body, you can take deliberate steps to alter the frustration into motivation. For instance, once you realize that the frustration is making you angry and is coming in the way of working at full potential, you can take a step back, calm down and tell yourself to brainstorm what frustrated you in the first place. By doing so, you will be able to pinpoint the cause of negativity and address it separately. With a fresh perspective and a surreal, more positive energetic vibration, we are much more likely to bring good into our lives, instead of bitterly repeating old mistakes.

I, personally, have seen many people who don't consider their words to carry any weight and that they have an influence on the quality of our lives. However, on the contrary, I have also met people who show huge consideration of their words and use them wisely.

If there's one thing our generation has lost the importance of, it's the impact words have, on our own as well as other's lives. Being legally blind has, at many occasions, given me the chance to observe this bitter reality very closely. Somehow, I was always seen as a disabled person and the way people talked to me was a mere reflection of their thoughts about me. It has become extremely commonplace to judge someone's disability and bully them for it.

Words have magical power. They can bring either the greatest happiness or deepest despair; they can transfer knowledge from teacher to student; words enable the orator to sway his audience and dictate its decisions. Words are capable of arousing the strongest emotions and prompting all men's actions.

Sigmund Freud, The Educator's Book

Words dictate how we are as a person and how we respond to all the worldly issues around us. Also, the words of other people seem to have a profound effect on us. What they convey to us and how they convey to us influence the energy we carry in ourselves. Spend a few minutes with a persistent complainer and you will see the change in your thoughts a while later. The person you are talking to will use all the negative terms, show you how unfair life is, and soon, you will find your energy in decline.

Words have the power to help, heal, harm or humiliate. If you try to relive your childhood or your past, regardless of your age, or the number of experiences you have been through, you must have a very vivid realization of your school days, those times when a tutor or the head of the school praised you in front of the whole school for getting a good grade on an exam or giving the correct answer to a question. You probably have a very fuzzy memory of your classmates, or what your teachers looked like, but there is just one thing that carries you through life. It is those words of encouragement and appreciation that you remember the rest of your life.

How many times have you thrown out your words without really giving them a thought? Being ungrateful about things and constantly expressing wishes creates a contradiction of energy in us. You all can probably relate to regular complaints like, "I wish I had long hair", "I wish I could travel across Europe" or "I wish I could be popular in school". However, what we fail to realize is that these constant wishes about what you want to have and not being grateful enough about what you do already have creates a big impact. It changes your mindset about how you see things. And the longer you delve into that pessimistic and ungrateful mindset, the worse it gets.

I, apparently, had to face the same choice in life. As I have already mentioned, I was born legally blind so I had pretty much to complain about, to constantly express my resentment and, could have had the "WHY ME?" attitude. However, I was fortunate enough to be able to control my thoughts from early on in life. I decided to do what was in my hands to be a better contribution to the world rather than a crybaby who is too obsessed with he does not have to care about what he has.

At school, I was always conscious about what kind of friends I want to hang out with, and so I always hooked up with people who had a positive impact on me. I always believed in what influence your surroundings could have on you and so I was keen enough to have grateful, ambitious, and well-to-do people in my circle of friends.

However, there was this one guy who was a gossiper, kept switching tables to spread all the news he could grab. Who is dating who, who puked in the class, who is cheating on who, the local teams match, that's all he could get his hands on? And so, he carried along with his business every day.

One day, he came up to me and said,

"Kyle, why are you so antisocial? You have nothing to say to all the news I share around the school".

Now, that really hit home.

How could he have such a harsh opinion about me when I have been in the least touch with him.

"I am not anti-social; I am just aware of who I want to b friends with. I am more inclined to have profound and meaningful conversations with the people I respect and get inspired from. I would rather spend an hour with nature instead of listening to what gossip you have to offer. I am pro-social when it comes to people, I want to follow the footsteps of."

Only when we are aware of the importance our words carry and the influence our words can carry on a person's well-being can we start to alter our habits to create a positive impact.

Here are a few tips to get started:

Enhance the sharing of positive things

We all are quick to share when something bad happens to us. However, when we get positive or good news, we refrain from sharing because we feel that the other person may not wish us luck or share our happiness. Get rid of this habit. As soon as you give more weight to your own emotions rather than how people will take them, your perspective will change and you will be more willing to share your happiness.

Resist from Gossiping

Avoid speaking ill of others as it results in your energy contraction. Even if you undesirably find yourself to be a part of gossip, try to turn it around by taking the conversation on a more positive track.

Avoid negative people

Limit the time you spend with people who do not bring out the best in you and find better friends. Negative energy has a way of dragging everything surrounding it in, like a big black hole.

Go on a negativity diet

Instead of boasting about a bad experience and using all the negative words to describe it, try to use positive words and instead say, "Maybe I will have a better experience next time".

You conveyed your point without having to use a negative word to describe it.

Offer Kindness

Don't be quick to judge a person. Always give them the benefit of doubt and try to empathize with what they must be going through before lashing out at them. Be a kind supporter instead of an authoritative boss.

Listen as much as you speak

Instead of always be willing to speak, give your fellow mates a good friend to talk to by listening to them.

"Good listeners, like precious gems, are to be treasured"
                                                            -Walter Anderson

Chapter 5

Power of Words and Thoughts

Through the previous chapter, we have firmly established the power of the words we say and the change that blossoms once we start altering the way of speech. We observed very closely that if we think and speak, it is almost as if the universe is there to answer and hear us. The words we utter determine the kind of vibrational energy that revolves within ourselves as well as in our surroundings.

However, another important aspect that works simultaneously with the power of our words is the power of thoughts we carry in our minds and the convictions we have.

It is often said that we are shaped by our societies and our present reality is just an outcome of the experiences we have has as a child, adolescent, and then an adult. Our thoughts that we have a firm belief in and that serve as the foundation for our future endeavors are all inherited by our family, peers, and friends. However, an interesting point to note here is that not one principle works for every individual. And therefore, when problems arise in our own lives, we have the power to change those perpetual thoughts into a mechanism that works more for ourselves than for society.

Our thoughts have the potential to change the current reality into a new reality. It is a very powerful concept and, at the same time, liberatory. Once we start questioning our thoughts and convince ourselves for some other positive thought that seems helpful, it eventually becomes true. What matters is that we can realize positive changes.

Freedom, happiness, richness, love, friendship, health, and wealth are our birthright. We all were born with free will, and only we ourselves have the control, and authority to change that free will into submission to someone or something. If our life is not what we dream for it to be, it's essentially because of the blockage in our thoughts. We may also say that the reason behind the kind of life we have is the thoughts that surround that life. Our thoughts are very powerful instruments that we can make tremendous use of, to either create happiness and wealth or sickness and poverty.

The best analogy that can help to understand the thoughts is that thoughts are like seeds. Just like you have command over what plant you want to grow; you have the same command over what kind of thoughts you want to adopt. Once you choose what plant you wish to have in your garden, you plant its seed. So is with each thought; you manifest the particular thought, whether positive or negative into your mind. Henceforth, you water the plant and give them fertilizers and eventually they grow. Your attention and enthusiasm are to thoughts what water and fertilizer is to a plant. The interest you show in a specific thought determines the growth of that thought into your mind.

"Whatever your mind can conceive and believe, it can achieve."
-Napoleon Hill

Thoughts, much like the seeds, have the natural tendency to blossom, gain firmness, and manifest into our lives. Using this natural tendency of thoughts brought about a positive change in our lives is a psychological approach, called Practical daydreaming.

The first step to Practical daydreaming is using your imagination to envision the kind of reality you desire. For example, you hope for a promotion at work but somehow you never achieve it. However, by using this approach, you can add a lot of details into that imaginary fantasy where you do get the promotion. Try to fill it with details like what will be the first thing that you do after you get the promotion. What kind of feeling will you experience and what kind of treatment would you expect from your friends and family once you share the news with them?

The second step is to filter out every possible negative thought from your mind regarding the imagination you desire to be a reality. Your primary focus should be how you want it to be and not what it could be. Eliminate all the undesirable thoughts like who would be jealous of your promotion and who would not wish you the best ahead in life.

Once the imagination is all about how you desire it to be and all the negative components are filtered out from it, the last step to this approach is to make a regular habit of repeating this imaginary reality in your mind once or probably more than once, in a day. Think of it as a mantra that you have to chant on a regular basis. You may be able to notice now that metaphorically, you have already planted the seed; you have picked out the weeds from the soil and are now watering it every day so it grows into a desirable output.

One essential clarity to have here is that this manifestation does not happen overnight. Many people have tried to make use of this technique but all in vain, only due to the fact that they are not consistent in their practice. As said, you need to treat this imaginary reality as a mantra until you start seeing the change in the true real world.

> *"Thought is a force – a manifestation of energy – having a magnet-like power of attraction."*
> **–William Walker Atkinson**

The research shows that we produce 60,000 thoughts in a day. We must be careful at every instant about what kind of energy those particular thoughts are sending into our minds and body. After all, by seeing how thoughts reflect our lives, we can easily conclude that there is a mind-body interaction. Mind continuously transfers the thoughts into our bodies and the accumulation of these thoughts can result in profound and meaningful revelations in one's life, if the thoughts are positive; and can also lead to destruction and ever serious mental illnesses, if the thoughts being accumulated are negative in nature.

Whenever encountering a difficult situation that puts you in dilemma between these negative and positive thoughts, stop for a minute and ask yourself, "What am I thinking about now? Am I making desirable thoughts or undesirable ones? What benefit they will bring to my spirit and body?" Once you have the answers to these questions, you can alter your way of thinking into creating a positive impact in your life.

Another way that is used extensively for spiritual healing is that of a pendulum. A pendulum is a tool that is believed to assist in many guidance measures by chasing the vibrational energy within you. However, one thing very important to note here is that a pendulum can answer questions in either a 'yes' or a 'no'.

For instance, you are trampled with confusing thoughts in your life, uncertainty all over you. You pick up the pendulum and place it between your index finger and the thumb and the pendulum and ask the question out loud, "Should I avail that job opportunity or turn it down?" Within a while, the pendulum will start moving with the help of energy within you. You conceptualize the movement of a pendulum so as to understand the answer behind the movement. The up and down vertical movements will indicate yes and the horizontal left and right movements will indicate a no.

Another method that has had a profoundly meaningful impact on me is the muscle testing technique. Muscle testing can give us insight into the inner workings of our subconscious in splendid ways. Not only does proper muscle testing allow us to identify the stresses and imbalances within our bodies, but since a majority of our physical, emotional, and mental processing occurs outside of our awareness, muscle testing is also an effective way to pinpoint key happenings at an unconscious level.

Muscle testing works in a way that it judges the movement of your muscles towards positive or negative and this way, you can conclude the answer. For instance, you are about to have the third cup of coffee in a day and you wonder if you really should. You place your arm straight in front of your body and ask the question out loud, "Is this coffee befitting to my health?" You, then very closely observe the changes in your arm muscles; if your body is swaying away from the arm, it's a 'no'. However, if you are leaning towards the arm, it's a 'yes'.

Muscle testing can also be witnessed by putting the arm straight and feeling the strength in your arm. Does it feel strong or is it limping? As you may take a guess, the strength in your arm shows a positive sign whereas the limping is a negative one.

I went to an allergist that used this method with all types of items to find out what might have been causing elevated inflammation. It was fascinating to me and something you might want to try out. I learned this from a lady I went to massage school with, and it was able to predict that we were going to have a daughter. Pretty cool huh?

A good life is the one where you are mindful of your thoughts. It is that tranquil state of being where you are fully aware of your emotions, thoughts, and feelings. Mindfulness helps you to regulate your emotions, which then turn out to be the biggest help in reducing depression and anxiety. It also helps to focus attention, as well as to discern conceptions and feelings without judgment.

Mindfulness is a constant practice that allows you to be present in the moment. The more you practice, the more you realize the importance of being in the moment. It gradually allows you to have control of your mind and emotions, instead of your mind controlling you.

The Reverend A.R. Bernard once said, "The quality of your thoughts determines the quality of your life". The quality of your life, as defined here, means the sum total of your health, happiness, vitality, leisure, and income which provides the food to your thoughts determines the quality of your life. It is because of your thoughts that you are at this point in your life, be it splendid or full of misery.

"Whether you think you can or cannot, you're right"

-Henry Ford

Your thoughts are ferocious; they have the immense capability to reproduce in the form you nourish them. They are invisible and yet, visible at the same time. It is invisible in a way that we cannot see them with the naked eye. Yet, visible because we constantly see the manifestation of our thoughts in our practical everyday lives. Your thoughts have the potential to take you to the skies if nourished properly, and throw you in the dumps, if not given attention.

There is a common saying that no one likes to hang out with sad and upset people because they bring out the worst in other people instead of pushing them to achieve their highest potential. Hence, we should surround ourselves with people who instead of taking every opportunity to bring you down use it to bring out the best in you.

Not only should we try to surround ourselves with these people, but also try to become one of them so that we are also one of those folks who are kind, humble, and fun-loving.

I firmly believe that doing things together makes just about anything easier and fun for everyone involved. Whether invited to a party, talking on the phone, or putting posts on Facebook, we share our energy and vibration with everyone we encounter. So, are we bringing our Wholeness, wisdom, and clarity—or are we bringing our worry, fear, and pain? For those who believe we want to be a positive force in the world, maybe it's time to claim full responsibility for everything we bring to the table.

The idea of claiming to take the responsibility of our thoughts was further embraced by Dr. Jill Bolte Taylor. She is an American neuroanatomist, author, and inspirational public speaker. In her interview at The Oprah Winfrey Show, she shared her experience of the times when she suffered from a massive stroke at the age of 37. The severity of the stroke exceeded to such an extent that within minutes after the stroke, she was unable to write, read, speak or even remember her mother. The only thing she could do was feel the energy of every person entering in her hospital room. Later, after many years, she wrote in her book, "I need people to take responsibility for the kind of energy they bring to me."

The host, Oprah Winfrey, was so touched by those lines that she put a sign in her dressing room that said, "Please take responsibility for the energy you bring into this space." She also spoke a few words of her own on the show and said, "Nobody but you are responsible for your life. It doesn't matter what your mama did; it doesn't matter what your daddy didn't do. You are responsible for your life. You are responsible for the energy you create for yourself, and you're responsible for the energy you bring to others."

Of course, it is fairly easy for us to spot this in other people. As the saying goes, some people brighten the whole room when they enter—others do it when they leave. We all have that friend or relative that sucks the energy out of every person at gatherings, and even when we know better, we often can't escape fast enough to not feel drained in their presence. Unfortunately, if we aren't careful, we not only absorb the toxicity but then turn around and spread it to others.

Having said that, the worst is yet to come; it is the point where we not only cease to take responsibility with our thoughts, we also start blaming others for everything that is not good with our lives. The problem with playing this "blame game" is that it blocks us from taking any possible constructive action. By deflecting responsibility for things, we get to feel righteous about our fear, anger, and pain rather than making any effort to see if we can change all or part of the situation. Anytime we believe that anything originates outside of ourselves, we are abdicating responsibility for thinking and acting. Don't believe me? Ask Viktor Frankl.

As you may recall, Viktor Frankl was an Eastern European Jewish psychiatrist who was held in a German Concentration Camp during World War II. There he suffered every sort of indignity and agony, including the loss of his wife and parents. Yet, later in his books and speaking appearances, he claimed that although the Nazis could impose every pain and torture imaginable upon him, only he could decide how he would act, react, and behave. Never does Frankl believe we should deny suffering and pain, but he does point the way to living above extremely difficult circumstances.

The purpose of quoting Jill Taylor, Oprah Winfrey, or Viktor Frankl is not to publicize their famous words, but to show my beloved audience, the importance of our thoughts and the changes that await you.

Section 3
Applying Your Wisdom

Chapter 6
Mental Health

As we all know, mental health is a paramount and unavoidable part of our health. Although mental health is not considered much pivotal in the world today, with the coming advancements and technology, it is becoming more and more clear how important this aspect of our life is and what repercussions we will have to face if we do not pay close attention to its development.

The World Health Organization defines mental health as, "a condition of complete physical, mental and social prosperity and not simply the absence of illness and sickness". However, a more important implication of this definition lies in the fact that health is more than just the absence of mental disorders or disabilities.

As opposed to the definition proposed by WHOM, mental health covers a diverse horizon of scenarios. To put it more accurately, mental health is the state of being, in which an individual can balance the stresses of life, his work, and family balance and also achieve his fullest potential while making a change in his community. This balance that allows him to perform his duties without causing harm to himself or anyone else can be called a stable mental state. It is a point of prosperity where individuals understand their capacities, adapt to the typical worries of life, work beneficially, and commit to their locale.

Contrary to a stable mental state, a mental illness is a physical illness in one or more than one part of the brain which then causes perturbations and thinking, behavior, energy, emotion that makes it difficult to cope with the ordinary demands of life. Research shows that a mental illness affects 19% of the adult population, 46% of teenagers, and 13% of children per year. The astonishing fact is that despite the large portion of the worldwide population going through such chaos in their lives, only half of those affected receive treatment. The mental health of every individual is fundamental. Society and the individual's capacity must act and associate with one another. The stigma against mental illness still seems to be on the uprise. This is largely due to media stereotypes and lack of education that people attach inaccurate myths with people going through these tough times.

This ferocious stigma against mental health is so robust that it not only hinders the appropriate treatment required for these people but also the number of resources available for their treatment. Although I must say that in the previous decade some powerful awareness has been raised regarding mental health, there is still a lot that needs to be done. Lack of resources available for treatment implies the lesser number of people who are willing to choose such professions, it can either be due to their personal bias or the restrictions imposed by their families against choosing a profession, "full of madness."

No matter how severe the stigma is, it seems to be commonplace in many parts of the world. Such stigma involves unfairness and discrimination because people attribute one particular characteristic to the personality of a person. For example, someone might be called a "psycho" or "psychotic" rather than "a person experiencing psychosis". This is one of many examples that are attached to mental since decades. This stigma not only makes the lives of such people worse but also causes the person to refrain from getting help because they think they will be judged and made feel left out.

Multiple factors play the role of triggers in such mental illnesses. For example, an abusive environment at home, lack of respect in marriages, stressful work conditions, unhealthy lifestyle, gender discrimination, and social exclusion are all possible triggers that can result in poor mental health. Physical health is given so much importance relative to mental health in the realm of science. Diagnosis of mental disturbances is more complicated than physical health. Unlike physical health, whereby if you want to build muscles, you have to start exercising, mental health is a lot more intricate procedure. There is no one-size-fits-all rule when dealing with mental well-being.

Mental strength is mainly composed of three main parts; thoughts, emotions, and behavior. Becoming mentally strong and developing resilience in the ups and downs of life requires a thorough regulation of your thoughts, the emotions associated with them, and henceforth the behavior.

It is critical to have your cognitive processes aligned with your behavior in order to be mentally resilient.

Create Your Form of Success

Those who are mentally strong will not feel called to enter into an unhealthy form of competition. This unhealthy form of competition specifically refers to competition with others. Mentally strong people know that everyone has a different definition of success and that, therefore, everyone follows a different path to success. They want to become a better version of themselves simply to improve themselves and achieve their dreams. In doing so, they create their specified definition of success and do not allow themselves to be influenced by others' opinions. They realize that they are unique and that it is okay to walk your path.

Challenge Yourself

Whether it concerns a personal or a professional goal; mentally strong people constantly challenge themselves and want to progress. They have clear goals in their lives that they want to achieve and that they enjoy working towards. They know why they set those goals and why that challenge is so important to their personal growth. It is important to evaluate and reflect on your progress. Are you going in the right direction? Can you still adjust something to achieve your goal?

Acknowledge Your Feelings

Whether they are sad, angry, happy, or ashamed; those who are mentally strong recognize their emotions. They will not minimize or hide their feelings from others because they know that they have to feel through every emotion to learn from it and move on. Emotions affect our thoughts and the way we behave, so you shouldn't ignore them.

Reverse Your Negative Thoughts

Everyone has negative thoughts from time to time. Surprisingly, also those who feel good mentally. The big difference between people who don't feel quite well yet and the people who do? Mentally strong people choose not to let negative thoughts take over. They are aware that this is about ideas and not about reality. They do this by thinking about where those negative thoughts come from and how they can give them a festive twist. Of course, everyone has a bad day from time to time, but how someone deals with that says a lot about that person's mental strength.

Use Your Mental Energy at The Right Time

Mentally strong people realize that the time they have and the energy they can invest in others is limited. That is why they use this mental energy at appropriate times and know when to spare themselves a little. They show it in not being concerned about all kinds of things all the time because they know that some things are beyond our control. They prefer to put that energy into matters that they influence, such as their personal growth.

Realize That You Also Have Shortcomings

However, we can do some things that do not apply to everything. Everyone is less good at something, and that's completely okay. Mentally strong people dare to admit that and face their shortcomings. Why? Because they know that they can work on this and that it is good to sometimes ask for help from others. Everyone has strengths and weaknesses, so everyone complements each other.

Take Your Responsibility

Stop looking for excuses and just take control of your own life. It's no more straightforward than that. Anyone who realizes that his behavior results from his own choices and how that behavior can influence specific outcomes is doing well. Mentally healthy people recognize that they are in control of their own lives and that they are in control. Break friendships that make you feel unwell and get out of that relationship that turned you into a shadow of yourself. That is becoming mentally stronger; realizing that this is your life and not someone else's. Take responsibility for your own life and start living it with your principles.

Chapter 7
Physical Health

Physical health is critical for overall well-being and is the most obvious of the various dimensions of health, which also include social, intellectual, emotional, spiritual, and environmental health. The purpose of stating the obvious is that it can be publicly observed unlike other states of being such as your mental health or emotional well-being.

A precise definition of a person who has good physical health is likely to have their bodily functions and processes working at their peak. This is not only due to an absence of disease. Regular exercise, balanced nutrition, and adequate rest all contribute to good health.

Physical health is a state of physical well-being, in which all our bodily mechanisms are at equilibrium with each other. It contains our lifestyle behavior, choices to ascertain health avoiding and preventing diseases, and live in an impartial state of mind, body, and spirit. Furthermore, regular exercise, a balanced diet, having adequate rest, cutting down on smoking, alcohol, and drug use is essential to physical health and mental wellbeing. You cannot achieve a perfect balance of your physical health by cutting down on smoking only. You need to have defined set rules to comply with in order to achieve your desired physical state.

To define a state of physical health, the physical activity of an individual would not be over-emphasized. Physical activities determine the state of physical health. Also, physical health includes potency, suppleness, and persistence. While your physical activities or exercise helps to enhance your health and reduce the danger of progressing several diseases like type 2 diabetes, cancer, and cardiovascular disease, physical activity can also have both instant and long-term health advantages. Most importantly, regular activity can improve your quality of life. Physical wellness promotes proper care of our bodies for optimal health and functioning. There are many elements of physical wellness that all must be cared for together. Overall physical wellness motivates the impartiality of physical activity, nutrition, and mental well-being to keep your body in a very good condition.

Many ways are being practiced to improve the physical self as we know it. Hydration, nutrition, massage, and getting in 10,00 steps. Adventures are some of the meaningful ways to bust your physical health. Another important thing to be noted here is that mental health also contributes to physical health. For instance, someone with poor mental capacity will then be less keen on having a balanced diet which will eventually impact your physical health as a whole.

EXERCISE

What is an Aerobic activity?

Through its definition, aerobic exercise simply means "with oxygen."

Aerobic activity is any exercise that includes any type of cardiovascular conditioning. It includes exercises like swimming, running, brisk walking, or cycling. They are all known as "cardio" because these exercises have a direct impact on your cardiovascular functioning. Aerobic exercise helps the way you breathe and your heart rate by increasing when practicing aerobic activities.

Aerobic activities have a lot of essential benefits to our physical mechanism; let's take a look at some:

Firstly, Aerobic exercises or activities are known for a reduction of the risk of diverse conditions, which includes high blood pressure, heart disease, obesity, type 2 diabetes, stroke, metabolic syndrome, and different types of cancer. Some weight-bearing aerobic exercises, which include walking, helps in decreasing the possibility of osteoporosis.

Aerobic exercise helps people with asthma lessen both the frequency and severity of asthma attacks. That's why a regular aerobic workout is highly recommended to asthmatic patients.

Research has also found that aerobic activities during the daytime aids in sleep and also regulates sleep. However, one should avoid working out near bedtime as it can disturb one's sleep routine.

What can be known as the difference between aerobic and anaerobic activity?

As said earlier, aerobic activity helps in quickening the heart rate and breathing rate to increase in a way that can be encouraged for the exercise period. While an anaerobic ("without oxygen") exercise is an activity that makes you to be promptly snap out of breath, just like lifting a heavy object.

So how prolonged should aerobic exercise be and how frequently can one practice aerobic exercises?

It is advisable for general health and fitness benefits, such as limiting the risk of heart disease and improving your stamina, it is suggested that you do some form of modest intensity aerobic exercise most ideally all the days of the week, for at least 30 minutes of a day.

The following listed are the best aerobic exercises for topmost health wellbeing.

I) Swimming

II) Outdoor cycling

III) Cross-Country Skiing

IV) Running

V) Jogging.

VI) Walking.

These are the types of exercise that help and benefit your heart and lungs greatly. These are more reasons as to why physical health education is introduced to schools, which has become a subject and field of study because it is so essential in our everyday lives.

And with the way physical health education has been introduced, one can define physical and health education as education, based on both learning about and learning through physical activity.

The benefits of physical education in schools are immense, including both increased student physical health and better academic performance. Conversely, a lack of physical activity among youth is known to increase the risk of obesity, cardiovascular disease, diabetes, high blood pressure, and more. By promoting physical education (P.E.) in schools, educators are in a prime position to help students establish life-long healthy behavior patterns and boost scholastic success.

Promoting physical education has been a hit idea for the students as well as the educational system. Students tend to be attentive in classes when they attend P.T classes. Research also suggests that physical training has a very impact on the students, some of them are:

Builds healthy bones

Improves strength and endurance

Reduces stress and anxiety

Helps control weight/reduces the risk of obesity

Improves blood pressure and cholesterol levels

Reduces feelings of depression

Boosts self-esteem

Promotes psychological well-being

NUTRITION

What is the basic definition of nutrition?

According to the "Advanced learners dictionary", nutrition is the process of strengthening or a means of benefiting specifically; the amount of the activity by which an animal or plant takes in by making use of food substances that are necessary for human nutrition.

Literally, food is an indispensable need for energy in the body. Food is any nourishing material that people or animals eat or drink or that plants consume in order to continue in life and advancement. What you put into it, is what you get out. Good diet and exercise go a long way to improving this.

However, the definition of insanity is continuing to do the same thing (eat the same things) and get a different result. I have seen many people around me who keep complaining of their increase in weight and yet continue to binge eat carbs and consuming cold drinks. This is precisely what insanity is and what leads to a negative set of physical health traits.

What are the six classes of food?

The six classes of foods are:

I) Proteins:

Proteins are said to be the ultimate players in the processes that allow an organism to function and reproduce. They are of great nutritional value and are directly involved in the chemical processes essential for life. Proteins are essentially found in molecules very large compared with molecules of sugar or salt and it consists of many amino acids joined together to form long chains.

The two main food groups that contribute to protein are the:

'lean meat and poultry, fish, eggs, tofu, nuts, seeds, and legumes/beans' group and,

'milk, yogurt, cheese and/or alternatives (mostly reduced fat)' group.

II) Carbohydrates:

Carbohydrates are macronutrients, meaning they are one of the three main ways the body obtains energy, or calories, the other two being proteins and fats. Carbohydrates provide fuel for the central nervous system and energy for working muscles.

Here are the groups of carbohydrates and some examples of where you will find the most of them;

Dairy

Milk, yogurt, and ice cream

Fruit

Whole fruit and fruit juice

Grains

Bread, rice, crackers, and cereal

Legumes

Beans and other plant-based proteins

Starchy Vegetables

Potatoes and corn

Sugary Sweets (Beware! you need to be cautious of this)

Soda, candy, cookies, and other desserts

III) Minerals: Calcium is mostly found in milk and other dairy products, also, it can be found in leafy green vegetables, egg yolk, and seafood.

Chlorine and sodium serve, amongst other roles, to keep the body hydrated.

Sulfur is an essential component of proteins and vitamins.

IV) Fats: Fat is a type of nutrient, and just like protein and carbohydrates, your body needs some fat for energy, to absorb vitamins, and to protect your heart and brain health. Fat is as essential to your diet as protein and carbohydrates are in fueling your body with energy. Certain bodily functions also rely on the presence of fat. For example, some vitamins require fat in order to dissolve into your bloodstream and provide nutrients.

Some examples of foods that contain fats are butter, oil, nuts, meat, fish, and some dairy products

V) Vitamins:

Vitamins are substances that your body needs to grow and develop normally. There are 13 **vitamins** your body needs.

Nutrient: Calcium

Food sources:

Nonfat and low-fat dairy, dairy substitutes, broccoli, dark, leafy greens, and sardines

Nutrient: Potassium

Food sources:

Bananas, cantaloupe, raisins, nuts, fish, spinach, and other dark greens

Nutrient: Fiber

Food sources:

Legumes (dried beans and peas), whole-grain foods and brans, seeds, apples, strawberries, carrots, raspberries, and colorful fruit and vegetables

Nutrient: Magnesium

Food sources:

Spinach, black beans, peas, and almonds

Nutrient: Vitamin A

Food sources:

Eggs, milk, carrots, sweet potatoes, and cantaloupe

Nutrient: Vitamin C

Food sources:

Oranges, strawberries, tomatoes, kiwi, broccoli, and red and green bell peppers

Nutrient: Vitamin E

Food sources:

Avocados, nuts, seeds, whole-grain foods, spinach, and other dark leafy greens.

The above nutrient classes can be categorized as either macronutrients (needed in relatively large amounts) or micronutrients (needed in smaller quantities).

What are the 3 types of nutrition?

There are two main types of nutrients, macronutrients, and micronutrients.

The three main classifications of macronutrients include carbohydrate, protein, and fat. While the two types of micronutrients are vitamins and minerals, and these are additional atoms that the cells need to form energy from.

So, with the above mentioned, we have been enlightened about the main reason why nutrition is so important.

HYDRATION:

As a massage therapist, I always encourage my clients to drink water before and after their session. It helps to circulate the lymph and stagnated interstitial fluid and flush any toxins out of the body. It also helps me during the session because it helps me to work less by making the muscles less dense. Clients are surprised when I tell them about their water habits based on my touch. Water itself has energetic properties as well. I even have a chart of the color of urine to determine how hydrated they are, hanging in the client restroom. The darker the urine, the more dehydrated you are.

Can you still be dehydrated if your pee is clear?

Drinking enough water each day is crucial for many reasons: to regulate body temperature, keep joints lubricated, prevent infections, deliver nutrients to cells, and keep organs functioning properly. Being well-hydrated also improves sleep quality, cognition, and mood.

How long does it take to rehydrate after dehydration?

The time it takes to recover from dehydration depends on how dehydrated you are. If you are severely dehydrated, it's likely that you will be hospitalized and be put on intravenous hydration for up to 24 hours to recover from dehydration, or until you're able to drink oral rehydration fluids yourself.

How does the body hydrate?

We collect the water in our body by drinking, and by dissecting the food during metabolism into carbon dioxide and water. The sweat, breath, and feces stay at the matching application, so the major command of body fluid content is passing through our kidneys.

What are the symptoms of dehydration?

They are:

I) Thirst.

II) Sticky or Dry mouth/tongue

III) Difficulty when peeing.

IV) Dark yellow pee.

V) Dry skin

VI) Headache

VII) Muscle cramps.

Most times, it is also advisable to take electrolytes. Electrolytes are vital to helping one regulate fluid balance. It also helps in controlling the blood pressure, helps the muscles compact, including the heart.

Here are the six electrolytes in our body namely sodium, calcium, potassium, chloride, phosphate, and magnesium. These are all electrolytes and we get them from the foods we consume and the fluids we drink. Also, it should be noted that the levels of electrolytes in the body can become too low or too high. This can happen when the amount of water in the body changes.

The following are healthy drinks abundant in electrolytes that can be consumed.

Coconut water or juice

Milk

Watermelon water (and other fruit juices)

Smoothies

Electrolyte-infused waters

Electrolyte tablets

Sports drinks

Pedialyte

But also, you need to understand that just like anything, too many electrolytes can be unhealthy. Also note that too much sodium is formally known as hypernatremia, which can result in dizziness, vomiting, and diarrhea. While too much potassium is known as hyperkalemia, this can influence your kidney function and cause heart arrhythmia, nausea, and an irregular pulse.

And how do you know if you need the electrolytes in your body?

The body generates cautions and signals beyond feeling thirsty when electrolyte levels drop, said by Dubos, a scholar. Fatigue, muscle cramps, nausea, and headaches can all point to either dehydration or mild hyponatremia, both of which permit an increase of an electrolyte intake.

SLEEP:

Do you even know that your body does the best healing during sleep?

Getting 8 hours of good sleep is beneficial. A lack of sleep at night can make you cranky the next day. And over time, skimping on sleep can mess up more than just your morning mood.

Getting a good night's sleep has enormous benefits for every age, some of them being:

BETTER MENTAL ACTIVITY:

When you're running low on sleep, you'll probably have trouble holding onto and recalling details. That's because sleep plays a big part in both learning and memory. Without enough sleep, it's tough to focus and take in new information. Your brain also doesn't have enough time to properly store memories so you can pull them up later. However, with adequate peaceful sleep, you will be able to retain more information and more efficiently.

HEALTHY EMOTIONS:

Another thing that your brain does while you sleep is processing your emotions. Your mind needs this time in order to recognize and react the right way.

BETTER CARDIO FUNCTIONING:

While you sleep, your blood pressure goes down, giving your heart and blood vessels a bit of a rest. The less sleep you get, the longer your blood pressure stays up during a 24-hour cycle. High blood pressure can lead to heart disease, including stroke.

MASSAGE:

Being a massage therapist, I would be remiss if I didn't include some benefits of massage especially of its healing properties in the parasympathetic state.

Benefits of Massage

1. It improves circulation2
2. It reduces muscle tension
3. It stimulates the lymphatic system
4. It is a means of relaxation
5. It increases joint flexibility and mobility
6. It improves skin tone
7. It improves soft tissue injury recovery
8. It reduces anxiety and depression

Chapter 8
Emotional Health

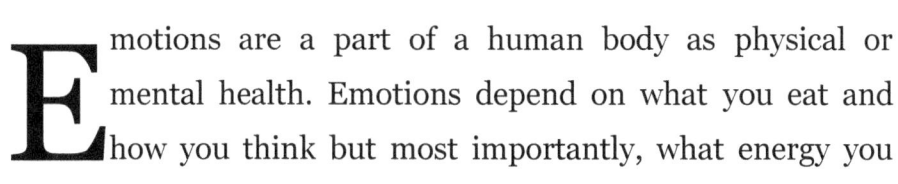

Emotions are a part of a human body as physical or mental health. Emotions depend on what you eat and how you think but most importantly, what energy you maintain. Emotions like joy, excitement, anger, sadness, guilt, betrayal are all part of us. It matters how we perceive one's experience and what story we tell ourselves.

Emotional health is an individual's ability to deal with feelings in different situations of life. Emotions tend to be too little, too much, or normal; it just depends on how much we understand ourselves. Let's say, a person is holding anger but never shows it because he never learned to express or let it go, what he did is suppressed his emotion and that is becoming a volcano inside that will burst with other coping mechanisms.

Emotions are required to be understood by one and nourished accordingly. We sometimes don't take emotional health seriously but in actual emotional fitness is as important for an individual as physical health. When we get a fever, we get proper treatment to get better as soon as possible whereas emotional health is always ignored by us which leads to long-term mental health problems like anxiety disorders, depression, behavioral disorders. There are three important factors to keep yourself emotionally fit, be resilient, positive, and focused. It is normally recommended to do inner cleansing by talk therapy, counseling, art, or connecting to nature. Exploring nature and thinking of nature as part of your identity can lead to emotionally healthy surroundings.

Parents play a vital role in a child's growth, if a parent disregards a child's emotion then that child's disturbance starts, time by time. For example, a child's anger initiated when he was not given support by his parent when he failed the exam. That's when it started, continued, and slowly steadily became a volcano. At the age of 45, that child feels disregarded inside. That's how emotions regulate and keep increasing if not dealt with and expressed in the right manner.

A person with good emotional health can keep the balance between various appearances of life and hence be able to maintain his physical, mental, spiritual, and sexual wellbeing. All these aspects of an individual are influenced by emotional health. It helps people in being optimistic in difficult situations of life and manages stress to enjoy life fully after that critical phase.

Research in the past showed that good emotional health can ultimately accompany success in all significant aspects of life.

This could be relationships, professional life, and so on. One will be able to do work towards their goals and fascinate others with their energy and optimism when their emotions are correctly expressed. So, it could be said that good emotional health is a key to success in life.

Another important factor in exploring emotional health is self-awareness. A person who is self-aware of his feelings can control their emotions according to the situation, navigate distress and validate their emotions fearlessly. The first step for navigating emotions is to have access to your true feelings by increasing a more personal connection with yourself. Some people are unable to do that hence end up taking counseling sessions and talk therapies to enhance their connection with their selves to make their life balanced and purposeful. Navigating emotions can guide people to take hold of your life in decision making and maintaining a successful relationship with yourself. Talk therapies and art therapies of counseling help people to keep track of their emotions and there is no harm in taking therapies from professionals.

Its natural human instinct to experience emotion as we live throughout our lives and it is very common for a normal human being to sometimes vent out in anger or be in an extremely happy state. Emotional health is all about your thought process and feelings, knowing your inner self and listening to your feelings can also lead to good emotional health.

Your emotional health significantly relies on the harmony within your body and the peace you carry within yourself. If you carry peace within yourself then your emotional health will be more likely to be in a better state and this way, there will be more chances to get connected with your higher self. The word higher self is very important to ponder here as it actually means the connection with yourself or in some ways it can also mean someone's relation and connection with God. So, the higher self is either your relationship with God or how better you know yourself.

Smiling:

The most common demonstration of an emotion a person can think of is a smile. Smiling has a lot of benefits in overall health but it has a great impact on maintaining emotional health. It is a human instinct to go through being sad, happy, angry, and various kinds of emotions in their day-to-day life but positive energy can be regained by keeping a smile on your face all the time. It pushes you to look at the positive side rather than focusing on the negative in every situation. Stress level can also be managed through this and in this way, you are making other's day beautiful too.

Connecting smiling to biological aspects, whenever you are happy about any positive happening in your life like getting a promotion or getting a new car, your body releases dopamine, serotonin, and other hormones that are responsible to enlighten your mood and overcome negative emotions. By smiling, one creates a very positive surrounding and stays productive and focused in professional life.

8 tips to improve your emotional self-awareness:

Step out of your comfort zone:

The first step towards the development of emotional health is stepping out of your comfort zone. Fear and negative emotions are a basic part of growing in humans but when you step out of doing the same thing you have been doing for life i.e., living in fear, it will make the path easier and emotional health strong. Suppose there's a person who works in a company as manager will explore nothing until and unless he will apply for some higher job and experience new things in life. So, getting out of your comfort zone is a key to reach the horizon of opportunities that will come in your way as you move forward.

People with weak emotional health, end up having problems in stepping out of their comfort zone. Deep down in their subconscious mind, they want to make their life purposeful by exploring new ideas but the constant fear won't let them do that. They are afraid to face challenges that could get in their way. The best way to say goodbye to your comfort zone is to aggressively challenge it. It's like going through all those scary things that kept on pushing you in your limited circle of comfort zone all of a sudden and then face the consequences accordingly. Making a mindset that there will be tons of negative outcomes you will be facing in day-to-day life as its natural process can also help in smashing the boundaries of comfort.

Identify and manage your emotional triggers:

A trigger is an incident that obligates an individual to react emotionally. For example, there's a person whose trigger is an unpleasant smell so whenever he has encountered a bad smell, he would show some emotion that most likely could be anger, sadness, or rage. When you identify your trigger, you will eventually be capable of protecting your emotional health.

Human encounters different situations in life where they show emotions regardless of thinking what people say about them and what would be its impact on their reputation. Have you ever thought why? What was the core reason for such emotion? Why do we need to cause such chaos and negativity? What you need to do here is go to a place where you feel positive and calm. For instance, if you sit back with a hot cup of coffee and a relaxed mind or go to a park to get some fresh air, you will be able to contemplate your trigger point. Try to think of your anger as a puzzle that you need to solve. Try to think, "Why did I react so harshly? What was going in my mind at the time I lashed out at my colleague? What kind of surrounding was I in?" By asking yourself these questions out loud in your mind, you will have a better understanding of your personality traits, emotions, and moods.

Moreover, be responsive to the difference between events that you can change and those that are beyond you i.e., things you can have a say on and things that are beyond your control. When you take a cab ride, tell the driver about your preferred route. When you order your favorite steak in the restaurant, ask for extra ketchup before the waiter leaves the table never to be seen again. You see, the two incidents I just described are events that you can easily control. However, you have less control over other events. Airplanes, for various reasons, are frequently late. As opposed to what you did in the restaurant, you can't call the pilot here and accuse him of being late. The only thing you can do here is to accept the delay as an opportunity to read or relax, not disastrous or worthy of anger.

When you will be capable of recognizing your emotional triggers, you will be very open to a conversation about them. It could be self-talk, or with a loved one, or a therapist. The first step will always be the same that is identify and manage your emotions accordingly. Learn to overcome these emotional triggers which are causing major complications in your life and ultimately you will be an expert to cope up with them. The load you carry within yourself needs to be addressed and thoroughly concluded.

Don't settle for things you don't want:

Very often, we face situations in our lives that make us feel very pessimistic. It almost feels as if something out of the blue has attacked us and has made our life very different. Call it discouragement, call it feeling down, or simply being unfortunate. You feel that you can't do anything right, and a dark shroud descends on the entirety of your considerations.

The interesting part here is that the problem is not the phase of sadness you are going through right now. The main issue that you need to address more carefully lies deep within. It arises when your mind starts seeing this temporary phase of misery as a permanent state of being. This is the time where instead of rebelling against the sorrow, you start getting comfortable with it. This is the critical time of your life where you are about to take a turn. Either you battle the sadness inside you or you welcome it with open arms only to realize later on in life what has it done to the bigger picture of your life. By welcoming this dejection, you are not only inviting more chaos into your life but also making it a long-term situation.

Therefore, the solution is to face it with all your might. Be aware that to fight in this state of depression, you need to be considerate as to what you can do and what you cannot. Again, it goes back to the same point I mentioned above about categorizing the possibilities and impossibilities. For instance, you have got a digestive disorder. Now, instead of seeing it as a long-term issue, blaming it on your destiny, and accepting it for the entirety of your life, you should tell yourself that, "It is alright. I have got this issue to deal with and I am doing what is in my hands to get over it. I cannot act as God to get rid of this illness in a second. There is nothing else I can do so I need to be patient until this bad phase completes its course and sees itself out".

Don't readily settle for things you wish for, either:

This is the opposite of what we just discussed. It is the human tendency to be overwhelmed by things that we have wished for a long time and once they become accessible, we go out of our way to get them.

Let me share an example here; there is a beauty concealer that you have been trying to get your hands on for a few months now. During these months, the imagination of getting that concealer has become so robust and vivid that when you find it in a store, you are not thinking even once before paying for it. What happens here is that the salesgirl took advantage of your desire for that beauty product that she lured you into the trap of buying half a dozen concealers. She might mention that these products are on sale and make you lose control of your mind and trapped you to buy more of that product.

However, there is a plausible solution to this as well. The solution is to not lose control and be conscious at all times. Don't allow another entity to get the best of you and lure you into their disastrous traps. Be present at the moment and think of all possibilities before making a decision.

Practice the art of self-observation:

Imagine your thoughts, feelings, or bodily sensations as clouds floating through the sky. Sometimes they're dark and angry; sometimes they're light and calm. But you are not the clouds. You are the blue sky who observes the clouds, without engaging. You simply observe them until they pass, and they will pass. Everything passes, good and bad. Be the blue sky. Be the observer.

For instance, on the off chance that you are a young man's parent and you need to serve them something decent for supper – vegetables and meat. You notice that he would not like to eat them and start letting out the food on the floor you just cleaned. You feel your fury rising inside you. However, if you "climb" over the circumstance, you will simply observe a parent who is concerned that their child ought to eat vigorously and get enough nutrients.

If you practice this regularly, you will create a sense of detachment when challenging situations arise. You will still feel it in your body, but there will be a space, and instead of feeling stressed or overwhelmed, you will be able to respond in a rational manner.

Work towards being the person you want to be:

Amidst the upheavals and shortcomings in life, we often tend to stray away from achieving the life we want and the person we want to be. We become so indulged with what we have and the responsibilities we have to take care of that we begin to forget what do we want from our lives.

What you need to do is take a quick survey and analyze your progress in life by answering these kinds of questions:

- » Is this vacation go into the heading I want it to?
- » Are my responsibilities expecting me to get things done with which I am not comfortable or happy?
- » Do my friends treat me how I might want to be dealt with?
- » Do I possess enough energy for my family?
- » Is my present path leading me to where I want to be in 2 years?

Test yourself to stay present:

Self-awareness is generally an interior cycle, yet there are outer ramifications of your inside circumstance. Start analyzing these usually to ensure that all is well.

- » How does your face look like?
- » Do you shave your face consistently?
- » Do your eyes look swollen?
- » Have you done your makeup today'?
- » What are you wearing?
- » Do you have clean garments?
- » Do they have wrinkles?
- » How does your work area look like?
- » Is everything clean?

- » Is everything in a significant heap of a jumble?
- » What is your stance?
- » Do you stroll with your face down?

Know about your typical self and be on alert for the occasions when you feel focused. Notice how everything changes. If you know about those changes, it may be simpler to distinguish the pressure factors later on before they arrive at your conscious brain.

Open up about your vulnerability:

We have always been taught in life that being strong and confident is good while being fragile and insecure is not. It is no wonder that we, as adults have learned to hide our flaws so well that we don't even know who we are anymore. So many people today are suffering from social anxiety, a condition that can be easily treated and cured. Yet, many are left untreated because of their unwillingness and inability to acknowledge as well as accept the issue as it would mean that they are exposed, vulnerable and weak.

However, it is high time we try to understand that there is not a faster and better way to personal growth than accepting and embracing our insecurities.

If we want to live a fulfilled life of realized potential and personal growth, we need to give in to the vulnerability and allow ourselves to feel weak and fragile, since it is also part of our nature.

Chapter 9

Spiritual Health

"If you knew without a doubt who walked beside you on this path you have chosen, you would never experience fear or doubt again." – **A Course in Miracles**

Spiritual health is all about having a determined and supernatural life. It is the achievement of distinct aspects and abilities of human beings. Spiritual health makes an equilibrium by connecting the physical, mental, and social sides of human life.

"Spiritual Health is also a determined life."

Spiritual health is achieved from spiritual practice that allows a user to believe that *"I am whole, perfect, and complete."*

What is spiritual health and wellbeing?

Spiritual health is achieved when you feel at peace with life. That peace is achieved when you find hope and comfort in even the hardest of times. It helps your experience life ultimately and from a broader perspective. However, the concept of spirituality is different for everyone. There is a vast difference between physical and spiritual health. The latter being associated with your perception of life and divinity. Spiritual wellbeing is achieved when you finally reach the levels of self-contentment and spiritual health in your life.

What is the importance of spiritual health?

Spiritual wellness acknowledges our search for deeper meaning in life. When we are spiritually healthy, we feel more connected to a higher power and those around us. We have more clarity when it comes to making everyday choices. Spiritual wellbeing allows our actions to become more consistent with our beliefs and values. It allows our thoughts, feelings, and expressions to flow as per our faiths and beliefs. Hence, allowing us to create a better version of our lives. Spiritual health allows you to understand your basic purpose of life and creation in a much better way.

The most important decision we make as humans is do I live in a friendly or hostile universe. All the rest is details." Albert Einstein.

Why are religion and spirituality important?

Both religion and spirituality can have a positive impact on the mental health of a person. Both of these directly or indirectly are linked with mental peace, self-contentment, self-belief, and personal growth of a person. These two concepts are coherently interlinked with one another so tightly that often their concepts are intermixed by the people. This is because of the commonality between the two. However, these two might be similar by theory, but when you go in-depth, they display totally different natures. For example, Both religion and spirituality can help a person tolerate stress by generating peace, purpose, and forgiveness. But benefits generally vary between the two due to their different nature.

ARE RELIGION AND SPIRITUALITY THE SAME?

Religion and spirituality are not always the same. Some people find their spiritual health in practicing religion. Others do not. It is whatever works for you. There is no right or wrong way to achieve spiritual health. In some ways, they provide the same impact. For example, both religion and spirituality can help a person tolerate stress by generating peace, purpose, and forgiveness. But benefits generally vary between the two due to their different nature.

Wayne Dyer once said this about religion, "It's not about being Christian, it's about being Christ-like. It's not about being Buddist but being Budda-like." You may have seen me use the word God and universe interchangeably in this book. But it doesn't really matter what you call it, it's the experience of the Spirit that is what really matters. Regardless of the religion, we practice, if any, we must demonstrate the values and beliefs that are part of the core fundamentals of it. After all, demonstration is what is most important. Actions speak louder than words.

What are some examples of spiritual health?

Spiritual wellness provides us with systems of faith, beliefs, values, ethics, principles, and morals. A healthy spiritual practice may include examples of volunteerism, social contributions, association to a group, fellowship, optimism, forgiveness, and expressions of compassion.

i) **Forgiveness:**
Forgiveness is a flow of energy. It helps you stay on course to peace by helping you avoid unresolved annoyance and problems. The common misconception about forgiveness is that people believe that forgiveness is letting go of a grudge or an incident. However, in reality, forgiveness has nothing to do with any person or situation. It's about you making an option to move forward with life. Forgiveness is about you, your mental and spiritual wellbeing, and your mental health.

"Forgiveness is not about saying what happened is ok, it's about letting go of the idea the situation could have been different" – **Oprah**

ii) **Gratitude:**

Gratitude means thanks and appreciation. Gratitude comes from the Latin word gratus, meaning "thankful, gratifying." When you feel appreciated, you're delighted by what someone did for you and also happy by the results. You feel blessed and gifted without feeling an obligation to pay back to that person. It replaces your responsibilities with gratitude and acceptance. Replace "I am Sorry" with "Thank You". It's a more selfless act.

iii) **Appreciation:**

Appreciation is a human feeling that can be most certainly defined as an acknowledgment of a selfless act. It reshapes life because it makes you cherish what you possess rather than fantasizing or dreaming of things you don't possess. Accordingly, thanking or gratitude mostly remakes your life because it is the solitary strongest source of creativity that any person can tap into.

If you clearly pay attention and look into things from a deeper perspective, you will find out that spiritual health is the actual depiction of beauty. It unlocks the mysteries of life, making things uncomplicated and easy in the longer run.

Here are a few other tips to improve your Spiritual Health:

MEDITATION

"It's the silence between the notes that make the music" –
Claude Debussy

Meditation allows a person to achieve a mentally clear, stable, and emotionally calm state. It allows users to train themselves to be more mentally aware and attentive. Meditation is necessary, for every person, as it allows you to see and comprehend things from a broader perspective by letting you tap into the secrets of life and your true self. Being mindful is a meditation on the outside.

SEVERAL KINDS OF MEDITATION:

MINDFULNESS MEDITATION:

Mindfulness meditation is a way of paying thorough consideration to the thoughts as they keep flying through the mind. The mind cannot be judged nor become involved with them. You can only watch and take note of any designs. This type of meditation is in conjunction with the application and alertness. It is also a way that helps to concentrate on an object while you continue observing bodily sensations, thoughts, or emotions.

Regular practice of mindfulness meditation has benefits for your physical as well as your mental health, including playing a role in the management of anxiety, stress, depression, sleep disorders, relationship issues, and eating disorders.

SPIRITUAL MEDITATION:

Spiritual meditation is commonly used in the eastern religions, regions like Hinduism and Daoism, and in the Christian faith. It is more likely to pray where you reflect on the silence around you to get an intense relationship with God eternal.

Spiritual meditation makes you realize the eternal truth and let go of all that had happened and will happen. The present is where you want to be and find solace. The need to practice spiritual meditation comes from an innate longing to see and think beyond the chaotic world surrounding you.

yOGA

Yoga is a centuries-old spiritual practice that means to make a feeling of association inside the professional through actual stances, moral practices, and breath development. The deliberate act of yoga has been found to lessen aggravation and stress, decline sadness and tension, lower pulse, and increment sensations of prosperity.

JOURNALING

Journaling is another frequently neglected, scrutinizing practice that can help you get mindful of your inner life and feel more associated with your experience and general surroundings.

Studies show that composition during troublesome occasions may be beneficial.

SURRENDER AND BEING IN NATURE.

Referenced in an earlier chapter, in 2005, I hiked 900 miles of the Appalachian Trail. This was one of the most meaningful periods of my life. For those that aren't familiar with it, It's a 2,100 mile footpath that goes from north of Atlanta on Springer Mountain, and goes to Baxter State Park in Maine. For most people it's quite a challenging venture to pursue and when you add someone with a visual impairment it's all the more challenging.

Everyone pretty much hikes their own hike. Some at a fast pace and some slower. I chose to take my time and enjoy the experience. Most of the time the people you meet you see for a day or two and maybe hear about them along the way.

My first couple of days I hiked with a guy called Vertical Eddie, which was his trail name. Mine was Happy Feet. I hiked with him for a couple of days and then he moved on, probably neer to be seen again.

A few weeks went by and I made it to Tennesee into the Great Smokey Mountain National Park. It was a touristy area with a lot of side trails and was hard for me to navigate through. One day, I was set to hike the highest point of the A.T., Clingmans Dome.

It was a long rainy day and I kept getting lost on side trails and couldn't find the main trail. It was getting dark and I was getting worried. Stuck on the side of the mountain miles from anything, I just set down on a rock and cried. "Lord, help me!" I cried. One minute later around the corner comes Vertical Eddie. "Hey Happy Feet, what are you doing here, the trail and shelter are just a half-mile up the way." With that, I was saved. Thank you, Lord.

The reason I'm sharing this story here is for two reasons. One, to stress the importance of being in nature. Just getting out in the world can be a very healing experience. I'm not saying everyone should go hike the A.T., but just getting out and getting your 10,000 steps in each day can help clear your mind. Or just lying in the grass can help ground you.

The second reason for this story is that sometimes you have to face challeging situations to get you to a place of surrender. We are not supermen and we don't have to take on the world ourselves. Sometimes we have to "let go and let God." Surrendering is not a weakness but an act of courage. It allows the Universe to collaborate with you to help carry the load of life.

One of my favorite lines in a song by Daniel Nahmod is: "if I stop steering my boat, does it sink? Oh no, a current carries it along just so. if I stop steering my life it's going to be alright I'll just go where the ocean says to go."

Chapter 10
Being of Service

There is a significant reason as to why I am concluding my book with this chapter. It's because this chapter is going to put an end to all that has been said and not only that, it will also explain what steps to take for the long run and how. It is a perfect essence of all the previous chapters.

There is a Chinese saying that goes: "If you want happiness for an hour, take a nap. If you want happiness for a day, go fishing. If you want happiness for a year, inherit a fortune. If you want happiness for a lifetime, help somebody."

For decades, many famous personalities have been preaching helping others achieve supreme satisfaction in life. Let us see what a few of them have to say:

For it is in giving that we receive
— **Saint Francis of Assisi**

The sole meaning of life is to serve humanity
— **Leo Tolstoy**

We make a living by what we get; we make a life by what we give

— **Winston Churchill**

*Making money is happiness;
making other people happy is a super happiness*

— *Nobel Peace Prize recipient Muhammad Younus*

*Giving back is as good for you as it is for those you are helping because giving gives you purpose. When you have a purpose-driven life,
you're a happier person*

— **Goldie Hawn**

Being of Service simply means rendering of assistance to something, someone, a group of people, a society, a belief — means that you've chosen to fix yourself with, without anticipating getting something in return. Being of service to something — a person, a group, a community, a cause, or a belief — means that you've chosen to engage without expectation of reciprocation.

Many times, I have witnessed people doing good only to find out later that there is some self-interest that is making them do the good deed. Celebrities often go to orphanages, old age homes and distribute food, clothes, and all essential items to the needy. No doubt it's a good thing to do, but what is the purpose of doing all that charity? It's because they know they will be attracting the local public and gain fame once pictures from their charity trip and reach out on Facebook and Instagram. They find their efforts worthwhile because they gain their self-interest very soon. It is easier to understand this by saying that these megastars would never do any charity of the sort, or never share pictures doing charity if there would have been no self-interest involved.

It would be unfair to say that only celebrities do this kind of charity to achieve fame. Nowadays, this form of charity that gives you benefit in return is almost seen everywhere and in everyone. It is very common-place to see a man helping his peers with the mindset that he will get something in return. And when these expectations are not met, people themselves from each other. This perspective of reciprocation associated with every good deed then leads to negativity, grudges and ultimately brings distance into the relationships.

When we think of kindness, we assume that it has to be some grand act in order to account. Not so. Something as simple as a gentle word, a smile, or a small token can dramatically impact another person in a positive way. No matter how it may seem on the outside, we're all dealing with something. Your kindness may make all the difference to someone who is suffering or going through a difficult time. Service is not about the size of the gift you give. Rather, it's about the size of your heart when you give. It's about your intentions and the ripple effect of doing well.

Current times make us live as if we are in a race, stressed, thinking about everything we have to do throughout the day, locking ourselves in our little world that does not let us see beyond our needs and desires, without being able to see what is happening around us and without the will to do so. Living inward makes us more selfish, giving way, at times, to states of loneliness, sadness, even depression.

With all the negative traits such as pride and vanity rising inside us, we lose the tendency to closely observe what needs to be addressed what needs our attention, where do we need to give our precious time and effort, and where will it have the largest and most fruitful impact. Just for the sake of a living, we forget about the true purpose of our lives, and instead, we keep running in the race that has no end.

When you have pride, vanity, and selfishness; it is difficult to put yourself in the shoes of the other. We feel that we are lowering ourselves before the possibility of help that may be presented to us. When thoughts of rejection assail us, such as: "How am I going to render my service to him if it is me, he should serve?" Ask yourself, "What do I get out of all this? What does this superior attitude give me in return?" It shows the moral inferiority that we have yet to be overcome because it can close any possibility of a good and healthy relationship.

We all have heard the name of Mother Teresa once or several times in our lives. In numerous social gatherings, I have heard this name being used as some sort of a joke, when one friend is asking another friend not to behave like Mother Teresa or at other times, a kind student being nicknamed as Mother Teresa.

However, only a small portion of the population seems to know who this great personality was.

Nun and missionary Mother Teresa, known in the Catholic Church as Saint Teresa of Calcutta, devoted her life to caring for the sick and poor. Born in Macedonia to parents of Albanian-descent and having taught in India for 17 years, Mother Teresa experienced her "call within a call" in 1946. Her order established a hospice; centers for the blind, aged and disabled; and a leper colony.

In 1919, when Mother Teresa, named Agnes by her parents at the time of her birth, was only eight years old, her father suddenly fell ill and died. In the aftermath of her father's death, Agnes became extraordinarily close to her mother, a pious and compassionate woman who instilled in her daughter a deep commitment to charity. "My child, never eat a single mouthful unless you are sharing it with others," she counseled her daughter.

With such great virtues instilled in her by her mother since childhood, Mother Teresa once said, "He, who does not live to serve, does not serve to live." We have to think that we are sociable beings, continuously interacting with the people around us. If instead of focusing only on ourselves and our little world, we learn to put ourselves in the shoes of the family member, friend, or a partner, we will be able to perceive the needs of those around us, to be able to help to the best of our ability. Sometimes our actions will be visible, but there will be times when they do not have to realize that we have given them that help. It is when we begin to live the virtue of service that we will increase other virtues such as humility, prudence, sweetness, patience, and charity.

As we mature, grow within ourselves, we understand how important the feeling of love is; we are feeling free from our apparent needs, the meaning of our life changes, awakening the desire to live, to help, to comfort, and to encourage the person who is close to us, going through difficult times.

The path that we are traveling while we learn to love all the people we can reach, known and unknown, teaches us to let go of our tastes and desires, diminishing our needs. In other words, we overcome the negative tendencies we have and increase the feelings that make us better people, developing sensitivity to the needs of others, feeling more united to them.

Selfless acts help us in all aspects of our lives, away from all the vicious virtues. If we do it with a deep feeling and show others that a life shared in love is more rewarding, more intense, that it fills us with joy and hope, it will encourage us to do things from the heart.

Mother Teresa of Calcutta: "Many times a word, a look or a gesture is enough to fill the hearts of those we love." Thinking that our work is going to affect another person predisposes us to fulfill our responsibilities and commitments to the best level we know because with our job well done, we also serve those around us, be it at a family level, social gathering, workplace, or solidarity level with the rest of the world.

In many places on earth, there are wars, cataclysms, hunger, injustice, and whatnot that people around the globe have to face. There are millions of people who need comfort or a hug, a little encouragement and support, a smile, or a little appreciation. If we put our minds to think that maybe there is someone who needs something that we can offer, for instance, food, shelter, some water, or maybe just a pat on the shoulder to show support. Every day is an opportunity that life gives us to be useful in society and make it a little better.

Teaching children to serve others is important because they learn very valuable attitudes about how to relate to other people, putting the needs of others before their own. Children who learn the value of serving those in need develop more authentic friendships and enjoy immensely their relationships with others.

"He who sincerely loves and charity is his principle of life, makes possible the works of the heart. Let's be good men and women; let's magnify ourselves with our daily work of internal transformation. In this way, we will do our bit to help change the world". So, let us not tire of doing well, because in due time we will reap, but we will not faint.

There is no private good. Energy is cyclical in all its forms and must flow just like water. You can't keep it all to yourself. You must be mindful where it goes and don't give away what you don't have, but it must flow through you, not to you, and then stop at a point.

If you can't help the homeless with money, can you help with a kind word or smile? You are never too late to help someone else if you are inspired to. Let your heart lead you. Once you are in a place of peace and you are in alignment, you have this overwhelming desire to share it. Like you discovered a secret that everyone should know or a restaurant that you like and you tell everyone about it.

When you ask, "How may I serve?" the universe responds with how can I serve you as well.

Epilogue

Don't just be inspired; Be inspiring

As of the writing of this book, we are in a global pandemic. Since the state of Oregon was shut down like the rest of the country I was also required to close my practice for a few months. During this time I decided to write. Even though it has been a stressful time for everyone I continue to remain blessed and continue to be grateful for everything that I have.

I hope that something you've read here has brought you some new insight. I hesitate to say inspire but rather to say that I hope that you are feeling 'in spirit".

It is more important to convey that I hope you are "in spirit" and are able to take that energy and inspire others.

Could you imagine being able to inspire others without doing anything? How would your life change if you become a highly inspiring person? Would you like to leave a mark on each person you interact with?

If your answer is yes, you are going to love yourself more.

Failures can occur at any point in time to anyone for any task, be it exams, jobs, or personal issues. In times of failure, many people tend to give up, many rise up and try much resort to unlawful activities again, and many start a search to find that ray of hope, which will inspire them to achieve their dreams without giving upon them.

In today's technological world, it has become easier to find inspiration, with the internet full of talks of successful people and motivational speakers, with movies giving life lessons and ways to live a happier life. You are depressed; you may just Google some videos to motivate yourself to go on in life. You fail an exam; you will get tons of videos on how to overcome your weaknesses and not get de-motivated.

Successful people are often seen advising and inspiring people to work harder, rise up after a fall, achieve their dreams, and much more. One listens to these talks and videos to stay focused and inspired. But how long can the effects of these videos sustain? Forever? Maybe not. That may be because we see the world through someone else's lens, paving our way by using the methods of others and getting habituated to be inspired by someone else every time we fail.

Why is it that we always need someone else to get inspired from? Why do we listen to stories of successful people and get inspired? Why can't we think of becoming an inspiration for someone else rather than vice versa? To get inspired is good, but to inspire someone is the best. We always look up to the records set by someone else rather than setting the records ourselves. If a task hasn't been done until now, we deem it impossible because someone else wasn't successful in doing it; we always search for ways to achieve success rather than creating one on our own.

In most of the inspirational videos by successful people, they mostly talk about their struggle and how they overcame the problems faced by them, be it financial troubles or people mocking them for dreaming big. This shows us that they did not need or were not waiting for someone to come and inspire and motivate them, they paved the way for themselves, and they succeeded in their ways and became an inspiration for others to see. We need to do the same; seeking inspiration would only give us temporary effects, but the desire to become an inspiration would stay forever and push us to struggle further and further until we achieve it.

So, go ahead, put off that inspirational video on the internet, move towards your goals, learn from your mistakes, pave your way for others to follow, don't give up, and one day you will become an inspiration for all others!

For me, being a person that is "in spirit" is very important as we are responsible for the impact we create. Only by inspiring others, you are already helping them to be better, and this is part of the purpose that we all have, don't you think?

There is no such thing as a disability, only obstacles. Our only limitations are the ones we hold in our minds. We all have obstacles; we all have things that disable us. The challenges we are going to overcome enable us to be creative and courageous enough to rise above them. I could focus on what I can't do, like drive a car or fly a plane. But instead, I highlight my accomplishments such as hiking the Appalachian Trail, running in the Portland to Coast, starting my private practice. Those are the types of Energy I want to resonate with.

Often when it comes to inspiration, it relates to artists or very creative people. In my opinion, we are all artists of our life, and we all, without exception, have the ability to become highly inspiring people.

For more resources and information about me, my blog, and podcast, you can visit my website at http://www.pleasantspirit.com or http://www.fosteringenergy.com

www.ingramcontent.com/pod-product-compliance
Lightning Source LLC
Chambersburg PA
CBHW070921080526
44589CB00013B/1391